# THE SOVEREIGNTY REVOLUTION

# The Sovereignty Revolution

**Alan Cranston**

*Edited by*
Kim Cranston

*With contributions by*
Mikhail S. Gorbachev
Jane Goodall
Jonathan Granoff
Jonathan Schell

**STANFORD LAW AND POLITICS**

*An imprint of Stanford University Press • Stanford, California*

Stanford University Press
Stanford, California
© 2004 by the Board of Trustees of the
Leland Stanford Junior University
Printed in the United States of America

Library of Congress Cataloging-in-Publication Data

Cranston, Alan MacGregor

The sovereignty revolution / Alan Cranston ; edited by Kim Cranston ; with
contributions by Mikhail S. Gorbachev . . . [et al.].
  p.  cm.
  Includes bibliographical references.
  ISBN 0-8047-4761-X  (cloth : alk. paper)
1. Sovereignty.   2. International relations.   3. Globalization.   I.  Title.

JZ4034.C73   2004
320.1'5—dc22                                                    2004004181

This book is printed on acid-free, archival-quality paper

Original printing 2004

Last figure below indicates year of this printing:
13   12   11   10   09   08   07   06   05   04

Designed and typeset at Stanford University Press by John Feneron in 10/15 Minion

*For* EVAN ALEXANDRA MACGREGOR PENNE CRANSTON,
*Alan's granddaughter, and future generations who represent
the beauty, love, and possibility of our world*

# Contents

# Acknowledgments

I know my father would want to thank many people who contributed in a variety of ways to this book. Unfortunately, among the many lists my father kept, I didn't find one for that purpose and can't, therefore, name everyone he would have thanked. I can, however, acknowledge the following people who, after my father's death, assisted in making his manuscript available to the public:

Sue Stanley, my father's able personal assistant, for keeping the master version of the manuscript for my father, for being of such tremendous assistance to me in incorporating final revisions my father made shortly before his death, and for providing copies of the final version of the manuscript throughout the publication process.

Zachary Allen, Associate Director of the Global Security Institute (GSI), for his outstanding and indispensable editorial contributions and assistance in bringing this work to publication. It has been a particular pleasure to work with him.

Ambassador Robert Grey Jr., Kath Delaney, Laura McGrath Moulton, Patrick Neal, and Carl Robichaud, present and past GSI staff members and interns, for their assistance in proofreading the manuscript and facilitating the publication process, and for continuing to advance my father's efforts to abolish nuclear weapons and increase global security.

My colleagues on GSI's Board of Directors for their support of this publication and for their continuing efforts to advance Alan's work to make the world safer for future generations: Colette Penne Cranston, Jonathan Granoff, Robert Klein II, Berniece Patterson, C. E. Pat Patterson, Kim Polese, Tom Rubin, Tyler Stevenson, and Lynne Twist.

My father's friends and collaborators who contributed writings to this publication, Jane Goodall, Mikhail S. Gorbachev, Jonathan Granoff, and Jonathan Schell, as well as Pavel Palazchenko, President Gorbachev's translator, for his dedication and his friendship.

Scott Sagan, Professor of Political Science and Co-Director of Stanford's Center for International Security and Cooperation, and David Cortright, president of the Fourth Freedom Forum and a visiting faculty fellow at the Joan B. Kroc Institute for International Peace Studies at the University of Notre Dame, for their tremendously helpful reviews of my father's manuscript and suggestions about its publication.

Alan C. Freeland for so generously giving his legal and strategic advice along the way.

Michael Green for his early contributions to this publication.

Carolyn Caddis for taking and giving us permission to use the photograph on the cover of this book.

The wonderful people at Stanford University Press for all they have done to bring this book to you, especially Kristen Brandt, John Feneron, Amanda Moran, Norris Pope, Puja Sangar, and Kate Wahl.

My father's sister, Eleanor Cameron, and his friends Bernard Rapoport, Vincent Ryan, and George Zimmer, who provided welcome encouragement in the lengthy process of publishing this book.

My wife and partner, Colette Penne Cranston, for reviewing and making great suggestions about the contents of this book, for her support and encouragement during the lengthy publication process, for all of her contributions as a member of the Board of Directors of the Global Security Institute, and for all of her other good deeds.

And my daughter, Evan, for her curiosity about Alan's work and the book, for being so understanding of the time I spent getting this published, and for all she is doing with her life to make the world a better place.

# Preface

A few days before my father passed away on December 31, 2000, he finished writing *The Sovereignty Revolution*. It contains his final thoughts on a subject for which he was passionate for most of his life—how can humanity effectively address the challenges we can only resolve at the global level, from international terrorism to climate change to regional wars and genocide?

He concluded that our current concept of sovereignty, which is "widely and unwisely thought . . . to mean only *national* sovereignty," was a significant factor in making the twentieth century the bloodiest in human history, and that humanity will not survive the twenty-first century unless our concept of sovereignty undergoes a revolution that acknowledges the primacy of the individual and emphasizes the importance of strengthening transnational organizations and international law. My father's lifelong passion for this subject led to his being sued by Adolf Hitler's agents for publishing an unauthorized version of *Mein Kampf* in 1939; to his writing *The Killing of the Peace*, which describes how a small group of people kept the United States out of the League of Nations and which *The New York Times* called one of the ten best books of 1945; to much of what he accomplished during his twenty-four-year career in the United States Senate; and to his continued efforts to abolish nuclear weapons after he left the Senate.

*The Sovereignty Revolution* is being published almost exactly as it was written at the time of my father's passing. Although a few small factual inaccuracies have been corrected, the manuscript has not undergone any rewrites or edits, as we couldn't know what suggested changes my father would have accepted.

The manuscript is being published with a Foreword by Mikhail S. Gorbachev, an Introduction by Jonathan Schell, and companion essays by Jane

Goodall and Jonathan Granoff. All were friends and collaborators of my father's whose perspectives were sought to enrich this publication.

In the final years of his life, my father continued to work to develop new approaches to resolving our global challenges, especially those posed by nuclear weapons. In 1999, he founded the Global Security Institute, which works to achieve incremental steps that enhance security and lead to the global elimination of nuclear weapons. It has developed an exceptional team that includes former heads of state and government, distinguished diplomats, effective politicians, committed celebrities, religious leaders, Nobel Peace Laureates, and concerned citizens. And in the last few weeks of his life, Alan inspired the creation of the Nuclear Threat Reduction Campaign—a joint project of Vietnam Veterans of America Foundation and The Justice Project—which educates and mobilizes key constituencies on a bipartisan, centrist basis to advance public policy that reduces the threat posed by nuclear, biological, and chemical weapons. Profits from the sale of this book will go to support such efforts and continue the work in which my father engaged to make the world more secure for this and future generations.

I often collaborated closely with my father over the years, and, since his passing, have frequently wondered what he would have to say about recent global events and trends, many of which he foresaw. I deeply miss his perspective and wisdom, and am happy to now share with you his final thoughts on the great issues of our time and the path he saw to a better human future. I hope that you will find value, as I have, in these thoughts, and that together we can all provide the leadership the world needs to prosper, not perish, in the century before us. I hope too that our leadership will be guided by the following observation of the philosopher Lao Tzu, which my father literally carried in his pocket for most of his life:

> A leader is best when
> people barely know
> that he exists.
> Less good
> when they obey and acclaim him.
> Worst when they fear and despise him.
> Fail to honor people

and they fail to honor you.
But of a good leader,
when his work is done,
his aim fulfilled, they will all say:
"We did this ourselves."

For all that you are doing to make the world a better place for this and future generations, I thank you and urge you onward.

Kim Cranston

December 2003

# Foreword by Mikhail S. Gorbachev

I met Alan Cranston in the second half of the 1980s—the years of Perestroika. As we set the goals of ending the Cold War and changing the direction of the international process from confrontation to cooperation, we were well aware that we could hope to succeed only if the initiatives of the new Soviet leadership were heard and its intentions properly understood. Alan Cranston was among those American political leaders who were ready to respond and to reciprocate. It was this reciprocity and the efforts of both sides that moved the process off the ground, particularly as regards ending the arms race. We concluded and ratified treaties eliminating medium-range missiles and cutting back strategic offensive arms. I am still convinced that those were truly historic achievements. Alan Cranston, as one of the widely respected and most experienced members of the United States Congress, did his utmost to make them a reality.

Alan was an ardent supporter of nuclear weapons reductions. It was his profound conviction that building up the arsenals of death is the wrong way to achieve security. His keen mind was at work seeking new ways and new approaches to the problem of security in our rapidly changing world. His involvement in these issues continued after his retirement from politics, during the years that brought us closer together. I had many opportunities then to appreciate his lively intellect, energy, and concern for the future of mankind as well as his commitment to democracy and dialogue. He was a frequent participant in the conferences organized by the Gorbachev Foundation, working particularly hard on issues of globalization and security. His remarks were always stimulating, revealing new aspects of the problems we discussed.

The subject of sovereignty in the new era, to which this book is dedicated, is one of the most complex problems challenging mankind at the turn of the century. It is a mix of conflicting interests and multiple issues, each calling for in-depth analysis. Alan Cranston was a true internationalist and was fully aware of the dangers inherent in unilateralist approaches, of attempts to achieve security without regard for the opinions of others—or even worse, at the expense of others.

International institutions, to which governments voluntarily delegate some of their sovereignty, were among the defining political phenomena of the twentieth century. They have played a prominent role in the settlement of international conflicts, providing a forum in which states representing different social systems and historical and cultural traditions worked together to solve common problems faced by all mankind.

Yet, today international organizations—and, indeed, all of us—need to respond to new challenges. If we are to deal successfully with the environmental crisis, the persistent, widening gap between rich and poor, the epidemics of new, previously unknown diseases, and finally the challenge of terrorism, we must work together, in concert. It is also clear that it takes strong states to confront a world in rapid transformation—and to strike a balance between sovereignty and the common good, between self-interest and universal interest. Failed states are becoming a source of and a magnet for various forms of extremism, including terrorism, as well as being incapable of giving their citizens a minimum level of security and a chance to live in dignity.

Globalization also confronts us with the problem of the limits of economic sovereignty and the governments' ability to act at a time when transnational corporations increasingly set the course of nations' economic affairs. Yet those same corporations are loath to assume responsibility for addressing the social problems of nations, for giving millions of people at least some protection in the face of blind economic processes.

These and other problems require thoughtful and responsible analysis. Political leaders need it the most, because the gap between the pace of change and the state of world politics is becoming dangerous. Failure to respond to it, adherence to the old ways of doing things, addressing problems primarily through the use of force, would lead us into a dead end, something that humankind cannot afford. As we look for new ways, we need the initiative of new generations and the wisdom of those who absorbed the political experience of the twentieth century. I hope that Alan Cranston's book will help readers in thinking over the complex issues that have no simple solutions and that call for a genuine, earnest dialogue.

Mikhail S. Gorbachev
December 2003

Strange is our situation upon the earth. Each of us comes for a short visit, not knowing why, yet sometimes seeming to a divine purpose. From the standpoint of daily life, however, there is one thing we do know: that we are here for the sake of others—above all for those upon whose smile and well-being our own happiness depends, and also for the countless unknown souls with whose fate we are connected by a bond of sympathy. Many times a day, I realize how much my own outer and inner life is built upon the labors of people, both living and dead, and how earnestly I must exert myself in order to give in return as much as I have received.

—Albert Einstein

# Introduction

JONATHAN SCHELL

A lan Cranston's life wedded idealism and practical accomplishment in a way that was perhaps unique in his time. As a four-term Senator from California, he pushed with relentless tenacity to help frame and strengthen the arms control treaties—the Strategic Arms Limitations Talks I and II, the Strategic Arms Reductions treaties, the Nuclear Nonproliferation Treaty, and the Comprehensive Nuclear Test Ban Treaty. These decades of public service within the formal political system were bookended by periods, at the beginning and end of his career, of equally intense political activity outside the system. Cranston was a participant in the famous Dublin Conference convened in October 1945 by Grenville Clark, the distinguished lawyer and adviser to presidents (and lifelong hero to Cranston), to establish the United World Federalists association. Cranston became the president of the organization in 1949, and left the post in 1952. Soon, in a radical shift from global to local concerns, he became the President of the California Democratic Council, which labored, with considerable success, to break the hammerlock that the Republican Party had on elected office in California at the time. This work led, in 1958, to his election as State Controller of California and, in 1968, to his election to the Senate, where he served four terms. His former role as president of the World Federalists was a possible liability in his election campaigns, but, as he liked to point out, he was protected from political damage by the fact that one Ronald Reagan had also been a member.

Did Cranston jettison his youthful convictions, growing more conservative as he grew older, as so many do when they enter the political system? He did not. Rather, he became more patient, working to achieve gradually the aims that he once had hoped to achieve all at once in the late 1940s. At the same time, he was learning. That the bold aims remained intact became clear in 1984 when, believing that the nuclear arms race was getting out of control in Ronald Reagan's first term, he made a brief bid for the presidency, running on a platform of nuclear disarmament. When that failed, he returned to his incremental work in the Senate. Then, after leaving the Senate in 1993, he returned to the nuclear dilemma, first as Chairman of the Gorbachev Foundation, and then as the President of the Global Security Institute, which he founded. It was in this period that he put together the Responsible Security Appeal, which calls for the abolition of nuclear arms, and was signed, at Cranston's urging, by such notable people as Paul Nitze, Gen. Charles Horner, and President Jimmy Carter. At an event launching the Appeal he said that although a nuclear arsenal "may have been necessary during the Cold War; it is not necessary forever. It is not acceptable forever. I say it is unworthy of our nation, unworthy of any nation; it is unworthy of civilization."

The riddle is how he managed to work on so many levels of political life at the same time, switching back and forth between them with the greatest ease. It was through his work on nuclear weapons in the last years of his life that I got to know him. One of the keys to his character was his modesty, which would have been notable in any human being but was simply astonishing in an elected politician. On his answering machine, he was "Alan," as he was to most who knew him. The human being not only had survived within the important official, it had grown and developed. Self-reference—not to speak of bluster or bragging—were at the zero level, as were all other forms of showmanship. Equally, there was zero variation in his manner toward the small and the great, the scruffy and the expensively suited. Sometimes I wondered how a four-term Senator could have managed this, and in the course of many days of travel and meetings together, I believed that I came to understand at least one reason. It certainly wasn't that he underrated himself, or failed to appreciate the scope of his ability or role. He had, for instance, a world-spanning rolodex and entree at every level of American and international life, and used these to the hilt in the cause. It was that his concentration, which was intense, was entirely on the work at hand. At every single meeting I attended with him, he made something happen, large or small. He passed along news, received news, asked for a further meeting, arranged one for someone else, won support for a project, or set a new project in motion—a job for someone, a research organization, an appeal, a television program, a film. He moved as swiftly as he moved quietly. The work was hard, intellectually as well as practically, and there just was no time for wasted motion, blather, or nonsense. Ordinarily, he was silent most of the time at meetings. He kept so imperturbably still—a gaunt Buddha—that sometimes I thought, "Well, a man of his eminence doesn't have to attend to every last word of every inconsequential meeting"—only to hear him speak up quietly at the end, summing up what had been said, making sense of it and offering suggestions, which usually formed the basis for what was done. Not for nothing had he been made Democratic Whip in the Senate.

What was true of his manner was true of his mind: it was, even in his eighties, fresh, resilient, receptive, reasonable, sensible, constructive, unburdened by conventional wisdom, unencrusted by habit, and crowned with what can only be called wisdom.

Alan Cranston died on New Year's eve, 2000. "The Sovereignty Revolution," complete but for a few details, lay on his desk. An outline for the introduction, in his characteristic block handwriting, was next to it. This essay, it seems to me, is the brilliant product of his singular evolution as a political man as well as a fresh, arresting, far-seeing synthesis of development of the security dilemmas in his lifetime. Though written before September 11, not one sentence of it is irrelevant to the post–September 11 world. Indeed, readers will be struck that right at the beginning of the essay he warns of a terrorist strike against the United States and specifically names Osama Bin Laden as its possible perpetrator and cites the first bombing of the World Trade Center as a precedent. At the center of the essay is the concept of sovereignty. Cranston had thought hard about this notion as president of the United World Federalists. From that point of view, of course, sovereignty, "widely and unwisely thought in our time to mean only *national* sovereignty with every nation supposedly supreme inside its own borders and acknowledging no master outside them" (in Cranston's words), was *the* great obstacle to a peaceful world constructed on federal principles. Nearly everywhere, he still believed, sovereignty, worshipped almost as "a god," is a focal point of strife, both between nations and within them, where it sets neighbor against neighbor. In the nuclear age, insistence upon the sovereign prerogative threatens the biological survival of nations and of the human species. Indeed, long before it was fashionable to do so, Cranston was traveling the country warning of the nexus of terrorism and nuclear weapons and the other weapons of mass destruction. In this essay, as in his speeches in the late 1990s, he quotes US Ambassador Robert Gallucci's warning that one day the United States might wake up to learn that terrorists had placed nuclear bombs in Baltimore and Pittsburgh, and were threatening to destroy these cities serially if the United States did not change its policies in the Middle East. Many Americans were shocked into awareness of these dangers by September 11. Cranston had woken himself up—and sought to awaken others—years before that terrible day. Had his advice been taken, it might never have occurred.

The thought of global terrorism was just one of the dangers, he believed, that demonstrated that the world of sovereign states was under challenge by global forces from without and splintering forces from within. His description of these forces, in a powerful *tour d'horizon,* requires few additions today. The idea of sovereignty, born in one age, had survived to prevent necessary action in another. It had lost most of its descriptive force and much of its prescriptive force. Many global corporations, he notes, have more attributes of sovereignty than many nation-states. As the title of the essay suggests, the transformation in question is not only one hoped for, it is one well under way. The question for him was whether the changes would occur consciously or blindly.

Cranston therefore wanted us merely to take charge of something that is happening anyway. In this respect, Cranston the elder differed from Cranston the young World Federalist. The World Federalists were revolutionaries, in the sense that they wished to lay siege to fundamental, immemorial, still-mighty structures of world politics and replace them wholesale with other structures. But in his later years, Cranston saw clearly that these structures were already badly eroded. So now he swam partly with, not wholly against, history's tide. At mid-century, the strength of states was little impaired; by century's end, they were weaker, and "immense disorder and worse can rise out of the weakness of nation-states if no workable way is found to solve global problems and to achieve global goals."

For guidance in the new situation, Cranston turned to an old source—the

Constitution of the United States—and a new one, the European Union. Sovereignty, the American founders held, was not the prerogative of a state but of the people. Political institutions were merely emanations of their inextinguishable power. It followed that the obstacle of sovereignty that stood in the way of federal plans—whether for the United States or for the world— could be surmounted. The people who created national governments could dip again into the reserves of their power and create international institutions. Nor did they have to make a choice between the two. The international institutions could co-exist with national ones, just as the American states co-existed with the federal government.

This much was consistent with the original principles of world federalism. The European Union added new lessons. For one thing, whereas the American constitution had been born, so to speak, in a big bang, the evolution of the EU was a study in incrementalism—a procedure more likely to be followed on the global level. For another, the EU is an association of full-fledged nations with histories going back as long as a thousand years—a state of affairs that resembles the plurality of nation-states in the world more than the comparatively homogenous collection of American states in the late eighteenth century.

In some respects, of course, the post-senatorial Cranston resembles the pre-senatorial one. The vision is still global. The habit of architectural thought is still present. But now, in a series of ingenious, deeply considered proposals, he wants to move gradually. These include proposals for gradually reforming the UN, adding strength to its institutions and infusing them with popular support that is the lifeblood of democratic politics. And he entertains the idea that it is no longer necessary to place mechanisms of global governance in just one location. Perhaps it will be found useful to create "a number of separate and distinct world institutions," which "may emerge as people and nations grope their way to a better managed world."

Like the life that lies behind it, "The Sovereignty Revolution" draws on a multitude of concepts and theories to create a new and richer coherence.

Jonathan Schell
December 2003

# PART I

# The Sovereignty Revolution

ALAN CRANSTON

# CHAPTER 1

# The Crisis of Sovereignty

I t is worshiped like a god, and as little understood.

It is the cause of untold strife and bloodshed. Genocide is perpetrated in its sacred name.

It is at once a source of power and of power's abuse, of order and of anarchy. It can be noble and it can be shameful.

It is sovereignty.

It is sovereignty widely and unwisely thought in our time to mean only *national* sovereignty with every nation supposedly supreme inside its own borders and acknowledging no master outside them, restrained but not necessarily much by international laws, treaties, and codes of civilized behavior, all of which are breakable and none of which are enforceable in the reasonably reliable and just way that laws are enforced in free and orderly nations.

Issues of sovereignty are involved in one way or another in all the forty savage conflicts raging today upon this turmoil-torn planet. They lie at the root of all the wars the United States fought in the late, unlamented, blood-drenched twentieth century that now mercifully lies behind us.

World War I began when the Austro-Hungarian Empire threatened the sovereignty of Serbia. World War II began when Hitler invaded the sovereignty of one country too many—Poland—and England and France belatedly realized that their own security and sovereignty were in danger. The Korean and Vietnam wars both involved the sovereignty designs of aggressive and ideology-driven communists in the north of each country versus anti-communists in the south.

Iraq's violation of the sovereignty of Kuwait led to the Gulf War. Saddam Hussein's blocking of the UN's search for weapons of mass destruction—on grounds of his own nation's sovereignty—led to the bombing of Iraq. Conflict between Serbs and Albanians over sovereignty in Kosovo led to ethnic cleansing, mass murder, and the bombing of Yugoslavia.

Today wars waged and violence perpetrated in pursuit of both newfound and ancient claims of sovereignty appear almost everywhere in the wake of the Cold War's end and the accompanying shattering of the uneasy, quasi-order it had imposed as it neatly divided nations into three camps: communist, anti-communist, and non-aligned. The fires of passionate crusades to achieve, assert, or defend sovereignty for one purpose or another or to avenge some breach of it light up the night skies of our time like some giant uncontrolled forest fire raging all over the world.

It would be an enormous oversimplification to suggest that sovereignty was the *only* cause of all these past and present conflicts. In a few it was, but other causes were involved in most—ideology, faith, doctrine, race, ethnicity, justice, poverty, ambition, power, territory, greed, resources, booty. Yet in every instance an assertion of sovereignty in the service of one or another of these or some other purpose was a vital element.

Some of the secessionist struggles to achieve sovereignty have been viewed as heroic, particularly those waged by people seeking to throw off the last vestiges of colonialism. Their struggles were elevated to a matter of high principle by Woodrow Wilson, who proclaimed "self determination" as a sovereign right in the course of the failed effort to establish enduring peace after World War I.

Sometimes a struggle to seize a piece of earth is based on little more than—as Joseph Conrad put it in *Heart of Darkness*—"taking it away from those who have a different complexion or slightly flatter noses." Sometimes it reflects a desire to establish a foothold on earth for oneself and one's brethren, a homeland in the sense suggested by Robert Frost: a place where, when you have to go there, they have to take you in. Whatever the cause, assertions of sovereignty felt to have been denied by history, or another ethnic group, or a different religion, or a hegemonic power, or something else—and defiant struggles to prevent these assertions by those seeking to preserve and protect present sovereignties—now threaten to disturb the peace of everyone everywhere.

Our own American continent is not immune from conflict and controversy over sovereignty, nor is our nation. To the south in Mexico a defiant Zapatista Army of National Liberation struggling for Indian rights in impoverished Chiapas has stood off over 50,000 government troops for years, while establishing "autonomous municipalities" in "liberated villages" and proclaiming that they are sovereign and independent. Mexico's new and independent president, Vicente Fox, is making conciliatory moves, and a peaceful settlement may be in sight. To the north in Canada there is non-violent but persistent separatism in Quebec where French-speaking people seek sovereignty.

No war has touched the territory of the United States since our own Civil War, combat with native Americans, a raid by Pancho Villa across our border, and the bombing of Pearl Harbor. However, hundreds of small but sinister militias and paramilitary forces have taken up arms in most of our states. They wave Nazi banners, burn crosses, commit hate crimes, and speak stridently of separatism in Idaho, Montana, and elsewhere. They engage in target practice in out-of-the-way forests and fields and threaten to turn their weapons on what they see as a remote and illegitimate US government that has stolen their sovereignty. These may be fringe groups that have failed to draw many Americans into their ranks, but we have already suffered several samples of the extreme mayhem a mere handful of violence-prone dissidents can provoke. There was the shootout with the FBI that ended in the massacre of the Branch Davidians at their compound in Texas. There was the siege and standoff between the FBI and the Freemen in Montana. There were the kidnappings and killings in the hills of Arkansas of citizens "whose names sounded Jewish" by white supremacists and separatists belonging to the Aryan People's Republic. And there was the bombing of the Federal Building in Oklahoma City that took 168 lives and injured hundreds more, perpetrated by a couple of disgruntled and disaffected Americans who view our government as an occupying foreign power. The weapons other angry Americans may wield in the future will not necessarily be limited to conventional bombs and bullets. An Ohio white supremacist, Larry Holmes, was caught trying to obtain deadly vials of plague bacteria—the infectious affliction that once wiped out half the population of Europe.

The bombing of the World Trade Center in New York was a direct and ominous import into our country of the terrorism creating so much havoc elsewhere, carried out by militant and fanatic Islamic radicals in retaliation for various perceived grievances including our intervention in the sovereignty struggles of the Middle East. Its toll was six dead, 1,000 injured. There are dark warnings of worse to come as terrorists proclaim they will wage a holy war against the United States and its citizens wherever they may be as long as we keep our "infidel" forces in Islamic lands in what they view as irreverent violation of their sacrosanct sovereignty by the "Great Satan."

Today more international terrorists lurk within the US and next door across the easy and open Canadian border than anywhere else in the world. The most infamous of terrorists, the wealthy Osama Bin Laden, who is estimated to have a personal fortune of at least $300 million to draw upon, has developed a worldwide infrastructure with cells in more than fifty countries, and is in a state of open warfare with the US. He is suspected of masterminding several attacks on American embassies and military targets abroad that have killed hundreds of people and wounded thousands. There is some evidence that his network was involved in the disastrous attack on the USS Cole in Yemen in October 2000. Sponsored and protected by rogues who have connived and powered their way to the leadership of states, terrorists have vast resources beyond those of Bin Laden behind them. And they seek weapons of mass destruction. So does Iraq, probably Iran, perhaps Afghanistan, Libya, and North Korea, and possibly other nations eager to acquire sophisticated weapons to offset the prowess and power of the weapons the US displayed in Kosovo and yearning to attain membership in the nuclear club recently joined by India and Pakistan.

The creation of nuclear weapons and their proliferation into many hands is the most ominous fact that emerged from the unflowered carnage and unforgotten sorrow entombed with the remains of the twentieth century. It separates today and all the tomorrows from all the yesterdays. Wars once had their limits. Despite whatever horrors humans experienced through the centuries, they have always been able to say, "Life goes on." That may no longer be an accurate assessment of the human condition.

Shortly after Hiroshima, I came to know Albert Einstein. He warned me as he warned others that if the power of these weapons was increased signifi-

cantly and if they were ever used all out, life on earth could be totally exterminated. The significant increase Einstein feared has occurred. There are
now roughly 32,000 nuclear weapons in the world with a combined power
equal to 416,000 of the now primitive bombs dropped on Hiroshima and
Nagasaki. A single twenty-megaton hydrogen bomb developed by the Soviet
Union could now unleash more explosive power than all that has been re-
leased by all weapons fired in all wars in all history. A man who knows these
weapons as do few others, General Lee Butler, who served as Commander-
in-Chief of the US Strategic Air Command during the end game of the Cold
War, observes, "We have invoked death on a scale rivaling the power of the
Creator."

Most people may tend to think that with the Cold War over and the Soviet Union gone, the danger that these weapons will ever be used has re-
ceded. Unfortunately, that is not the case. The *sad* fact is that it is more likely
now that nuclear weapons will be used than it was during the perilous but
more stable era of the US-Soviet arms race. An accidental or unauthorized
nuclear exchange between Russia and the United States—a distinct threat
throughout the Cold War—constitutes an even graver danger today, given
the chaos in Russia, the declining command and control her civilian and
military leaders have over her weapons, and the bristling nuclear arsenals still
kept on a state of hair-trigger alert by both countries and subject to instant
launching in accordance with two dicey Cold War nuclear doctrines—
Launch on Warning and Mutual Assured Destruction (otherwise known as
MAD)—upon which both nations still inexplicably rely.

The pleasant assurances vouchsafed by President Clinton and President
Yeltsin that the United States and Russia no longer target each other are
symbolically nice but substantively insignificant. The US and the USSR both
deliberately singled out targets in the heart of each other's principal cities
during the Cold War starting with the Kremlin and the White House—
insuring the deaths of millions of civilians living and working nearby if the
weapons were ever fired. These original targets still reside in the memory
banks of the missiles of both countries. It would take only a few seconds and
a few swift strokes on a computer to zero back in on the Cold War targets.
Worse, expert testimony heard by Congress indicates that if the missiles are

ever fired accidentally, Russia's would automatically retarget while in flight, and would still destroy American cities.

A deliberate terrorist attack is a more likely eventuality. Former US Secretary of Defense William Cohen, a Republican, warned in 2000 that a terrorist attack somewhere on American soil with chemical, biological, or nuclear weapons is "probable" within the next ten years. His Democratic predecessor, William Perry, says of the use of weapons of mass destruction, "It's not a question of *whether* but *when* and *where.*" General Charles Horner, who commanded Allied Air Forces in the Gulf War, and former US Ambassador Robert Gallucci, who engaged in nuclear weapon negotiations with both Iraq and North Korea, both expect an American city to be subjected to a nuclear attack sometime in the next ten years. Gallucci describes how it could happen:

> One of these days one of these [rogue] governments fabricates a couple of nuclear weapons, and gives them to a terrorist group. The group brings one of these bombs into Baltimore by boat, and drives another one up to Pittsburgh. And then the message comes in to the White House. "Adjust your policy in the Middle East, or on Tuesday you lose Baltimore, and on Wednesday you lose Pittsburgh." Tuesday comes, and we lose Baltimore. What does the US do?

What does any nation do?

The tragic consequences of any such deed, wherever it might occur, will not necessarily be any more confined by national boundaries than is the global flow today of information, money, and drugs. After these ghastly weapons have destroyed their targets and snuffed out the lives of nearby men, women, and children, fatal radioactive fallout can seep across the borders of nations with invisible and silent stealth, like a gas stove giving off its lethal hissing as we sleep, its deadly destination determined more by the whims of the winds than by malevolent human intention.

No one is immune. Nowhere on earth is there a safe haven.

Although the magnitude of the risks now facing everyone are unprecedented in all the long history of humanity, this is not the first time that humankind has experienced such periods of achingly hollow chaos and seemingly all-encompassing political, economic, military, social, and spiritual upheaval amidst revolutionary eruptions of discontents. Some two thousand years ago, Tacitus described a terrible time in Roman history as "rent with sedition, gloomy with war, and savage in its very hours of peace." In the more recent years that witnessed the slaughter of World War I and the butchery of the Irish rebellion against England, the great Irish poet William Butler Yeats penned these lines:

> Things fall apart; the center cannot hold;
> Mere anarchy is loosed upon the world,
> The blood-dimmed tide is loosed, and everywhere
> The ceremony of innocence is drowned;
> The best lack all conviction, while the worst
> Are full of passionate intensity.

Today unrestrained passions and impulsive quests for new identities, powers, and independence explode in country after country and on continent after continent, driving the shattering and splintering of the world like a historical force of nature impossible to tame. Potential clashes and conflicts loom on a scale surpassing those that are already causing so much havoc and so many deaths of innocents.

## The Balkans

A mere glance at the world around us reveals with shocking swiftness the ominous nature of the gathering forces of fragmentation and the chilling extent of the rising perils they pose at the dawn of the new millennium. Starting in Europe at the dividing line of the old Iron Curtain and moving eastward, the scorched earth already left by violent and momentous change is first encountered where it has devoured the lives, property, boundaries, and fate of the former Yugoslavia, now the site of several new and struggling states including war-ravaged Bosnia, Croatia, Slovenia, and Serbia, where UN forces now stand wary guard amidst smoldering ethnic, cultural, religious, and sovereignty hatreds and aspirations.

The worldwide uproar provoked by the atrocities perpetrated in Kosovo, the consequent bombings launched by the US and the other NATO nations, and the storm and stress this created in relations between China, Russia, the US, and other major powers are warning enough of the vulnerability of all humanity to the costly contagion that can spread so far so fast from a single struggle over sovereignty.

### The Former Soviet Union

To the east in the vast space once ruled by the Soviet Union, fifteen new and independent sovereign republics have been born, not without heavy cost in lives, blood, tears, and pulsating heartache in those where civil wars and general strife exploded in the aftermath of the Soviet breakup. Georgia, led by the respected but beleaguered former Soviet Foreign Minister Eduard Shevardnadze, has had to contend with the armed sovereignty-seeking struggles of two ethnic enclaves, Abkhazia and South Ossetia, and with threats from a Russia deeply resentful of Georgia's independence and still maintaining military bases on Georgian soil. Soon after the republic of Moldova achieved independence it was torn by a conflict pitting its minority of ethnic Russians against its majority of ethnic Romanians. Muslim Azerbaijan and Christian Armenia have been in a steady and savage struggle over conflicting claims to the mountain territory of Nagorno-Karabakh ever since the restraining hand of the USSR vanished. And in Tajikistan combat between fundamentalist Muslims and other forces has been muted to some extent only by the anti-Islamic and despotic iron rule of its former communist leaders who still hold sway and by 11,000 Russian troops stationed there. There is sporadic strife between Islamic guerrillas and government forces of two nearby republics they seek to destabilize, Kyrgyzstan and Uzbekistan.

Relations are tense between Russia and several more of the new republics where former Soviet troops, now Russian, remain or stand forebodingly on their borders. Russia and Ukraine, the two largest states to emerge after the implosion of the communist empire, seemed on the verge of war in the early years of their independence, and the sovereignty of Ukraine still is looked upon by some in Moscow as an insult, a humiliation, and a loss that should be remedied by force.

Myriad potential internal rebellions brew across the vast expanse of the territory of Russia itself, spread across the map from Moscow in the west and ending thousands of frozen miles and eleven time zones away at the Bering Straits on the Pacific. Russia is made up of eighty-nine so-called "semi-autonomous republics," regions, and ethnic statelets. Any of them could be tempted to demand complete separation and full sovereignty. They all already elect their own parliaments, and their own presidents or governors. Several have established their own military forces. One governor, the strong-willed General Alexander Lebed of Krasnoyarsk, has hinted he may seize Russian strategic nuclear missiles that are stationed on his territory. Many of these semi-nations maintain "embassies" in Moscow and have negotiated "treaties" with the Kremlin. Most evade paying taxes levied by Moscow and ignore edicts issued by the Kremlin. Boris Yeltsin once urged them to take on as much sovereignty as they could swallow, but that was before he became president of an independent Russia and suddenly acquired an interest in holding his country together. His successor, Vladimir Putin, has launched an ambitious attempt to curb their powers.

The most defiant republic, Chechnya, has been struggling for independence from Russia ever since it was invaded by Ivan the Terrible more than 400 years ago. It launched a Muslim-led war of independence shortly after the demise of the Soviet Union that claimed 25,000 lives and bequeathed in its wake only shattered cities and blood-drenched soil when a humiliated Russia finally withdrew its battered troops, leaving a ruined, chaotic, and crime-ridden Chechnya to stew in a surreal and shambled sovereignty that was its in every way—except that no formal recognition of it was ever admitted by the Kremlin. There was only a short lull in the fighting before it flared anew when rebels from Chechnya showed up next door in the autonomous Russian republic of Dagestan to launch a struggle to overthrow the government there. Their apparent aim was to set up an Islamic state and to drive Russia out of the Caucasus entirely. This was more than Russia could put up with, and troops were sent back to Chechnya. Once again they received stiff resistance from undaunted Chechnyan fighters and strong criticism from a western world appalled by the brutality of the battles and its countless civilian casualties. The civil war rages on.

## China and Her Neighbors

Of larger potential import to the world is looming turmoil to the south and east of Russia. The two most populous countries in the world, China and India, both possessors of nuclear weapons and between them comprising more than one-third of the world's population, face not only separatist strife within their own borders but also possible collisions with each other and with other neighbors over matters of sovereignty.

There is a presently slumbering but potentially massively destructive clash of claims between Russia and China over who is sovereign in large and disputed territories separating the two giants along their common border. This unresolved dispute provoked a brief military collision in 1969 between the Soviet Union and China despite their shared communist ideology. A Russian Governor, Eugeny Nazdratenko of Primorsky Krai, recently imprudently fanned the flames by challenging the present border demarcations and ordering his militia to harass Chinese traders. A Russian scholar, Enders Wimbush, compares "the inviting emptiness" of the vast stretches where Russian sovereignty presently holds sway with the teeming Chinese "hordes" on the other side of the border. He notes reports in the Russian press that "the concern that this region will be overwhelmed by Chinese is increasingly evident." A sign that the US is concerned about the potential for trouble here surfaced in the summer of 2000 when the US Air Force conducted war games based on the international situation that would hypothetically develop if a "rising large East Asian nation"—obviously a prudently unnamed China—tried to wrest control of vast Siberia and all its gold and oil from a weak Russia.

The rulers of China must themselves worry about growing agitation for territorial independence inside their own domain. Terrorist bombs are being exploded, government officials are being relentlessly and systematically killed, and separatists are being summarily executed in the vast province of Xinjiang. There have been anti-government riots in the city of Yining near the border with Kazakhstan. These disturbances are believed to have been fomented by Islamic radicals who resent living under the domination of Han Chinese and who want to break away from China and form a Muslim state. Another Chinese nightmare has the people of its province of Inner Mongolia seeking to secede and merge with the bordering sovereign nation of Mongolia, a fledgling democracy that was once the home of one of all history's greatest marauders and violators of sovereignty, Genghis Khan. Meanwhile, China's fierce determination to hold by force the once-sovereign land of Tibet causes trouble with other powers. The People's Liberation Army suppressed a full-scale Tibetan revolt in 1959, and brutally crushed pro-independence rallies mounted by Tibetans in 1987–89.

## China and Taiwan

The dangerous dispute over Taiwan's status goes on and on, with China refusing to rule out the use of force to put an end to the suggestion that Taiwan is separate and sovereign. An actual Chinese invasion may be unlikely, but if it ever did come it could well spread and involve Japan, South Korea, and other nations. The US has been resolutely ambiguous about what it would do if China actually initiated military action to take over Taiwan, but it is generally anticipated that the US would move to the island's defense. A Chinese general suggested to a US official that if the US did so, China could bomb Los Angeles in retaliation.

Other political and economic pressures within China raise the specter of its possible implosion in a manner similar to that which shattered the Soviet empire. Senator Daniel Patrick Moynihan has pointed out that China has not one but five races—the dominant Han, plus Manchus, Mongols, Tibetans, and Uighers—and "contains fifty-six so-called National Minority Peoples, numbering some 90 million persons and inhabiting more than 60 percent of its territories." This diversity is clearly one of the major causes of the political repression by China's communist leaders, who are fearful that they, like their late counterparts in the defunct Soviet Union, will lose their total personal grip over China's sovereignty.

## India and Her Neighbors

Nearby India, already the largest democracy on earth, is on its way to surpass China to become the most populous of all nations. The territory of Aksai Chin was torn away from India by China in the 1962 war between the two giants, and who possesses title to other land along their common border is still disputed. There are serious nuclear tensions between the two countries, and these are aggravated by careless Indian boasts that their country has a hydrogen bomb capable of destroying Chinese cities.

Today's India has many of China's internal characteristics of diversity and potential divisiveness, starting with the deep differences that divide its 87 percent Hindu majority from its 11 percent Muslim minority (a small component percentage-wise but large enough numerically to make India the third largest Muslim nation). India's billion people communicate—or don't communicate—in seventeen major languages and more than 22,000 distinct dialects. Different states mandate different official languages. Linguistic, ethnic, and religious minorities carry on age-old separatist activities, some peaceful, some violent. The violent sort led to the 1984 assassination of Prime Minister Indira Gandhi by Sikhs angry over unsatisfied demands for separate religious recognition, linguistic rights, and sovereign autonomy in Punjab, and to the assassination seven years later of her son and successor as Prime Minister, Rajiv, apparently by Sri Lankan separatists. The ever-burning issue of sovereignty in Kashmir has caused three wars and threatens a fourth between India and Pakistan. It was a major factor in the decision of both nations to test nuclear weapons in 1998, imperiling the non-proliferation efforts of the international community. Another potential cause of chaos and combustibility lies in the unpleasant fact that India has as many as 500 million illiterate and poverty-stricken people.

### Indonesia

The world's fourth most populous country, after China, India, and the US, is Indonesia, and there, too, the people are splintered religiously, ethnically, and economically, with enormous potential for separatism and conflict. Java, the hub of this chain of more than 13,000 Pacific islands that make up this illogical country inhabited by 250 ethnic groups speaking 500 tongues in an archipelagic Babel, is highly civilized and advanced. In Irian Jaya, however, at the tribally minded western half of New Guinea where separatist agitation is on the rise, the men still wear loincloths and the women grass skirts. Student activists demonstrating for independence in Jakarta and in oil-rich Aceh Province on the Muslim island of Sumatra triggered the events that led to the overthrow of President Suharto in 1998.

Widespread bloodletting, maiming, and killing were endemic for years in East Timor's struggle to escape repression and retrieve the independence it lost when it was invaded by Indonesia in 1975. The post-Suharto government allowed the Timor people to express their wishes in a 1999 referendum that was marked by shooting, burning, terror, and killing inflicted by anti-independence thugs and militia gangs sponsored by Indonesia's armed forces. The people defied their tormentors and voted overwhelmingly for full independence rather than autonomy within Indonesia. The Indonesian parliament ratified the verdict, and East Timor will soon join the family of nations, but it is now a temporary ward of the UN. The ward is still beset by sporadic violence that has spread to the province of Maluku, once known as the Spice Islands, where Muslims have taken to killing Christians and Christians to killing Muslims, and runaway local police and rogue militias go on bloody rampages. The Indonesian government is considering granting some form of decentralism and federalism that would give all the provinces control over their resources and some autonomy—a move bitterly opposed by angry patriots who hold to the nationalist credo, "One Country. One People. One Language."

## Sri Lanka

These profound upheavals are not, of course, confined to the giant nations of the world. The infectious nature of the spreading plague of fragmentation is demonstrated strikingly in Sri Lanka, a young country that after more than four centuries of foreign domination achieved independence without violence when the British Empire let go in 1948. The diverse people of Sri Lanka have actually cohabited peacefully for 2,500 years, but in the 1980s their immunity vanished as they succumbed to the separatist virus and fell into what has now stretched into two decades of brutal conflict between the government and insurgent Tamils who seek sovereignty. The struggle has become particularly painful for the children of Sri Lanka as the rebels have taken to raiding schools, orphanages, and homes to forcefully recruit boys and girls, some not yet ten years old, who are handed guns and forced into combat.

## Afghanistan

In Afghanistan, a country ravaged by more than twenty years of constant warfare, the issue of who will ultimately exercise sovereignty after the debacle of the Soviet invasion and withdrawal still causes blood to flow. The merciless Taliban, after overthrowing the puppet regime left behind by the departing Soviet forces, are slowly consolidating the power of a new fundamentalist Islamic state that practices medieval punishment, treats women abominably in accordance with edicts officially promulgated and enforced by the notorious Ministry of Vice and Virtue, and gives sanctuary somewhere in Afghanistan's remote mountains and deserts to terrorist Osama Bin Laden.

## The Middle East and Africa

It seemed conceivable in 1999 that peace efforts might at long last bring surcease to the tormented lands of the Middle East with their long and tragic history of warfare, terrorism, and deathly donnybrooks over sovereignty in Jerusalem, sovereignty in the Gaza strip, sovereignty on the Golan Heights, sovereignty on the West Bank, sovereignty in Lebanon, sovereignty here, sovereignty there. High hopes were crushed in 2000, however, by a new outbreak of violence. The turmoil is unabated, though there is a faint and lingering hope that some sort of shared sovereignty arrangement in Jerusalem might produce a breakthrough.

Not far away the ancient and unrequited aspirations of the Kurds for a state of their own are harshly repressed in the three nations among whom they are dispersed, Iraq, Iran, and Turkey. Then there is the massive bloodshed and suffering that has sent so much of Africa into tears and its people into the common tombs of mass earthen pits in Angola, Burundi, Congo, Rwanda, Sudan, and elsewhere on that explosive, impoverished, and AIDS-ravaged continent, so much of it still awakening to the trials and turmoil that accompany new and varied sovereignties as they seek haphazardly to emerge.

The worst African war, with a death toll approaching two million, has embroiled six nations, three rebel forces, and several militias in Congo. The worst of many tribal conflicts have been the massacres committed by Hutus attempting to exterminate Tutsis in Rwanda. Atrocious, too, has been the slaughter in Sierra Leone, where an eight-year civil war has been provoked in good part by a compelling compulsion by those who yearn for diamond mines to take them away from whoever has them. The struggle has left two million homeless and countless dead. It has also left many thousands of crippled civilians and their crippled children whose hands and feet have been hacked off as a matter of deliberate terrorist policy by rebels wielding machetes in a sinister movement known as Operation No Living Thing.

A legacy of countless amputees similarly characterizes the long, long civil war in Angola. In this case the amputees are not the victims of a deliberate policy but rather they are the random result of the many land mines carelessly strewn around the country. All told, the Angolan conflict has left another two million Africans dead or displaced. The principal contestants wrap their respective crusades in confusingly similar slogans of sovereignty that suggest that their purposes are purely patriotic. One side calls itself the Popular Movement for the Liberation of Angola, while the other calls itself the National Union for the Total Liberation of Angola. Actually the struggle seems to be largely fueled by the matter of who will possess the vastly rich oil fields of this country that is sometimes called the Republic of Chevron. The struggle was complicated and confounded for decades by the shifting sands and alliances of the Cold War. The US once supported the rebels against the government but now supports the government against the rebels. The Reagan administration sued a major oil company, Gulf, for doing business with the government the US now supports. The oil company's operations were guarded and protected at the time, despite the aroma of capitalism surrounding them, by troops furnished by socialist Cuba.

There are hostilities in Sudan that have taken almost two million lives— more than Bosnia, Kosovo, and Rwanda combined—in a war waged by the governing National Islamic Front against the country's minority Christians and animists who when captured are often sold into slavery. There are hostilities in Namibia, a spillover of the war next door in Angola, as Angolan rebels cross the border to retaliate with violence for the Namibian government's aid to the Angolan government. There are hostilities in Somalia where for years there was total anarchy and no national government at all, and also no significant religious or ethnic disputes, but where instead warlords and clans joust locally for bits and pieces of territory, and where much of the violence is more criminal than political. A transitional government was finally chosen at a conference participated in by 2,000 delegates from Somalia's clans and held in Djibouti, a small neighboring country. The warlords refuse to recognize the government, and so do two self-proclaimed autonomous regions.

The most baffling and inexplicable African battle, yielding tens of thousands of dead, pitted two of the world's poorest countries, Ethiopia and its former province of Eritrea, against each other. Much of this pointless struggle was waged over whose sovereignty would prevail in barren borderlands and a remote, unknown town called Badme that will be of no economic or strategic value to whoever winds up possessing it. A cease-fire negotiated late in 2000 may have finally ended this senseless conflict, but just where the boundary lies between the two countries has not been agreed.

Africa was subjected for many years to an arbitrary and ruthless order imposed upon it by colonialism, and then to some extent by the Cold War. In the disorder that has followed, we now behold a continent consisting of 2,000 tribes speaking over 500 dialects in fifty-three countries whose illogical borders, drawn arbitrarily long ago by the colonial powers, are almost totally irrelevant to the individuals and tribes living within them. Each tribe has its chief who relishes the power his family may have held for centuries. More than one chief now has visions of leading a separate and sovereign tribal nation.

## Western Europe

Conflicts over issues of sovereignty large and small churn on interminably elsewhere. Western Europe now seems to be a relatively calm oasis in a stormy world, yet even it has its separatist troubles. They range from Britain's long history of combat with the bomb-happy Irish Republican Army to the kingdom's voluntary "devolution" of significant authority—but not of independence—to the Scots and the Welsh after both voted in referendums for a degree of autonomy. Sentiment for full separation and independence appears to be rising in Scotland. France has its share of separatist strife due to the activities of what has been called a "curious mix of shepherds and bomb throwers" on the island of Corsica, while Spain has had to contend for thirty years with the rebellion of irrepressible Basque secessionists whose independent-minded ancestors gave similar trouble to the Roman Empire two thousand years ago. There are also bitter sovereignty disputes between Greece and Turkey over the divided island of Cyprus and in the Aegean Sea.

## Latin America

Latin America has been more or less free of combat since the end of the Cold War and with it the subsiding of the strife it did so much to stir in El Salvador, Guatemala, and Honduras. An exception, however, is Colombia where the large and lucrative traffic in drugs finances a remarkably wealthy guerrilla insurgency and has led to constant gunfights and killings with no end in sight. Whether the government or criminal drug syndicates run the country is a subject of vigorous debate, and so is the murky question of the relationship between high government officials and drug kingpins.

## Elsewhere Around the World

Around the world other small and not-so-small struggles storm on. There are hostilities in the Philippines, with Muslim terrorists—allegedly armed with weapons from the Middle East and inspired by fanatic Islamic preachers who were trained in Egypt, Pakistan, and Sudan—tossing bombs and grenades night and day amidst kidnappings and assassinations. There is even trouble in paradise. An armed coup d'état erupted in the languid Fiji Islands, usually envisioned as a South Pacific Shangri-La. The coup was spurred by animosities between the 40-something percent of Fijians who are Indians

and the 50-something percent who are native Melanesians, but it also re-
volved around laying hands on mahogany, land, and money.

There are hostilities and fears of new hostilities threatening to break out
in other places, too many to mention.

Most of these conflicts directly disrupt and destroy only the lives of those
who live in their midst. Some spread and envelop others in other lands. It is
clear that even the most powerful nations are not immune and that, taken
together, the conflicts pose perils for all humanity. There is always the danger
that a single conflict, in a single land will draw others in, striking sparks and
scattering the flames and fires of terrorism, chaos, and combat anywhere and
everywhere. And conceivably leading inadvertently to a worldwide nuclear
holocaust.

# CHAPTER 2

# Sovereignty Redefined

Dangerously unexamined in the midst of all this is the true meaning of sovereignty.

Few of the combatants pursuing this holy grail that they proclaim as the rightful reason and holy purpose justifying their often unholy exertions, and all too few of the rest of us, have given much if any consideration to the real nature of sovereignty, its history, and its explosive implications for the human condition. This is a failure on our part and an absence of thought which promises only the gravest of consequences.

Professor Louis Henkin, the renowned Columbia University authority on international law, who has probably thought as deeply as anyone about sovereignty, has written:

> [Sovereignty's] birth is illegitimate, and it has not aged well. The meaning of sovereignty is confused and its uses are various, some of them unworthy, some even destructive of human values. . . .
>
> The pervasiveness of that term is unfortunate, rooted in mistake, unfortunate mistake. Sovereignty is a bad word . . . not only because it has served terrible national mythologies; in international relations, and even in international law, it is often a catchword, a substitute for thinking and precision. . . . For legal purposes, at least, we might do well to relegate the term to the shelf of history as a relic from an earlier era. . . . As applied to a State, elements long identified with 'sovereignty' are inevitably only metaphors, fictions, fictions upon fictions.

In the beginning, when the first humans appeared on earth, their individual sovereignty was virtually absolute. They were truly *free*. They could climb the trees and walk beside the rivers and make their way across the plains and through the jungles virtually unchallenged by other humans. They had to cope with harsh forces of nature and ferocious beasts, but not with any government.

This original sovereignty in a state of nature slowly vanished through the unnumbered generations in the ever-enlarging scale of human social development. We will never know just how countless changes unfolded in that impenetrable time, but it is plausible to imagine that unspoken social contracts were gradually entered into as the primitive decision-making of individuals—their personal sovereignty—came to be shared with or seized by mates, families, tribes, clans, chiefs, councils of elders, and that the first dim glimmerings of something akin to government slowly emerged over the eons and took on a few of the shreds and later some of the substance of sovereign authority. Much of this only began about 10,000 years ago, when humans, who had been nomads for their first hundreds of thousands of years on earth, began to settle down and cultivate the soil. They then slowly gravitated together in villages, villages gradually grew into towns, and towns into cities, and these also had their leaders and their rulers.

Over the many millennia of human and social maturing, as consciousness and capacity slowly evolved over the interminable ages, countless forms of human relationships and governance were tried, discarded, and tried again. Religions, superstitions, ideologies, and ambitions were born and died, drew people together, drove them apart. Civilizations rose and fell, but through it all, issues of sovereignty—who was in charge and who wasn't—largely told the tale.

Recent archeological and paleoanthropological unearthings have yielded evidence—primarily in the nature of the weapons that have been found and in the broken bones in well-preserved skeletons—that in prehistoric times people settled their differences with little violence and lived together and with their neighbors in other communities more or less peacefully until about 6,000 years ago. The change may have come when wandering humans who had originally been hunter-gatherers settled down to be farmers, and eventually acquired land and other resources over which to quarrel. The Seville Statement on Violence, a report submitted to UNESCO in 1986 by distinguished scientists from many disciplines and many lands, concluded

that biology does not condemn humanity to war. Specifically, they concluded that it is scientifically incorrect to suggest that we inherit a tendency
to wage war from our ancestors, wrong to believe that war and violent behavior are programmed into human nature genetically or by evolution. Professor William Ury of Harvard University, an anthropologist whose findings
about how our ancient ancestors worked out their differences turned him
into a modern day negotiator, comments, "This myth that human beings
have been killing each other most of the time for as long as they existed—
that it's our basic nature and if you scratch the veneer of civilization you get
a Bosnia or Rwanda—is fundamentally mistaken."

We know that eventually conflict did come, and that it embraced more
and more people as their leaders struggled with each other over land, posses-
sions, power, religion. All too much of history is unhappily told in terms of
wars, conquests, victories, defeats, and the power to rule that went, however
briefly, to the victors. Conflicts between unknown and long forgotten villages were followed in time by conflicts between city-states like Athens and
Carthage, precursors of today's nation-states. Conquests led to larger territories presided over by emperors, empresses, kings, queens, khans, grand vi-
ziers, and others with exalted titles. These rulers came to be known as "sovereigns," many of whom sought to enhance the legitimacy of the limitless
authority they exercised over their subjects by asserting that they ruled by
divine right bestowed upon them by God. They claimed to be blessed with
"sovereign immunity," a doctrine of privilege that put them above the law
since under it they could not be prosecuted no matter how savage their
treatment of their subjects. Sovereignty in this stage of its development be-
longed to individuals—but only to the privileged few who seized or inherited
it, not to the unprivileged many who had none.

The origins of the modern system of sovereign nation-states are generally
traced back to 1648 and the Treaty of Westphalia that ended the Thirty Years
War. The treaty embodied an agreement that the royal rulers of Europe's 300
kingdoms, principalities, and baronies would recognize the absolute sovereignty of each in his own realm. Each anointed leader would have the right to
handle affairs in his own territory in his own unfettered way without outside

interference. The sovereign equality of each ruler and his state with each of the others was to be accepted, regardless of discrepancies in the actual size and strength of their domains.

Professor Stephen Krasner of Stanford describes the Westphalian system as "Sovereignty: Organized Hypocrisy" in his recent book bearing that title. For in fact the treaty by no means put an end to meddling by the rulers in each other's affairs, and did not end the incessant wars between them as the strong conquered the weak and swallowed their lands and their subjects. The 300 domains dwindled in number, with the survivors commanding increasingly large territories.

It was not long, as time goes, before abuses of power by those who had acquired so much of it led to unrest among the people, to the French Revolution, and to a new concept of sovereignty. Sovereignty came to be seen as belonging not to individual rulers and their dynasties, but rather to nations. This principle was proclaimed in the new French Republic's 1791 constitution. It declared, "Sovereignty is one, indivisible, unalienable and imprescriptible; it belongs to the Nation; no group can attribute sovereignty to itself nor can any individual arrogate it to himself."

This new sense of national sovereignty and the spirit of democracy and the hunger for human rights and freedom that it sprang from slowly spread from country to country. The elites whose powers and privileges were threatened by this new and heretical concept did their utmost to obstruct it. Progress was interrupted from time to time by coups d'état, counterrevolutions, and the seizing of power by little and large Napoleons, Lenins, and Hitlers, but nation-states slowly became the chosen instrument for the assertion and establishment of human rights, as well as for the governing of territories and people.

Professor Henkin has concluded that—regardless of whether a nation is a democracy or something else—the essential characteristics and indicia of a sovereign state today include principally "independence, equality, autonomy, 'personhood,' territorial authority, integrity and inviolability, impermeability and 'privacy.'" He accompanies his definition with the caveat that these elements of sovereignty as applied to a state are inevitably only "metaphors, fictions, fictions upon fictions." They may now become even more illusory and fictitious as surging globalism threatens the authority of individual nations.

Today we live in a world that prides itself on the progress of democracy. As recently as 1900, there was not a single country where the most fundamental standards of democracy were fully met. In no country then were the people able to choose their governments in free elections in which every adult was allowed to vote and more than one party could participate. The US, England, France, and a handful of other countries were certainly democracies, but even they fell short of those basic standards. Now, a century later, however, the people of 120 of the world's 192 countries meet them, while the people of a good many more have attained democracy in more limited forms. Most authoritarian regimes have been replaced by governments that are more responsive to the will of the people, although a number of these are imperiled by corruption, lack of well-established institutions of democracy, and lack of leaders and citizens adequately devoted to and experienced in the ways of democracy.

Yet despite the forward march of freedom and the manifold benefits it brings to people who have a choice in how and by whom they are governed, democratic processes today are playing only an insignificant part in two mighty and seemingly contradictory developments that are shaking and shaping our world.

One is the separatism, the fragmenting centrifugal force that is pulling us apart. The outcome of most of the struggles over sovereignty is largely determined not by ballots but by bombs, bullets, terror, and torture.

The other is globalization, the integrating centripetal force that is pushing us together. Globalization has provoked little violence thus far, but apoplectic, red-faced protests are erupting in country after country over a claimed, presumed, or humiliating "loss of national sovereignty" to this faceless, dreaded, homogenizing force feared or thought by many to be overpowering our identities and our freedoms, and much more. There was a hint and a taste in the streets of Seattle of what might be in store when foes of globalization disrupted a meeting of the World Trade Organization late in 1999. President John Sweeney of the AFL-CIO has warned that Seattle will look "tame" if the conditions that provoked the protests are not dealt with. It is not yet clear whether globalization will lead to cooperation or conflict.

It is quite clear that the governments of nations are finding it frustratingly difficult to make decisions for, against, or about globalization. It is the creation not of governments but of transnational corporations, multinational banks, supranational speculators, multimedia conglomerates, and the remarkable new masters of the Silicon Valleys of the world as they capitalize on the modern miracles of science and technology. Their primary purpose is materialistic. Their focus is on capturing markets and reaping the profits they promise, although many of them believe—some of them quite correctly—that they are enhancing the comforts of life for countless individuals and families. The dimensions of the business they do and the influence they wield is staggering. At last count about fifty corporations had a greater net worth than most countries.

These goliaths seek no formal sovereign authority, but they are having a profound effect on the sovereignty of nations. National borders become steadily less meaningful as a trillion dollars a day and more flash electronically in nanoseconds from corporation to corporation, investor to investor, country to country. National currencies rise and fall at the incomprehensible whims of invisible others. Information, ideas, pornography, tips on where to get drugs or how to make bombs seem to flow anywhere and everywhere on the virtually unaccountable, unfettered, wildly free phantom of the Internet that is making new connections between people all around the world. The once sovereign capacity of nations to exercise control over such matters appears to be fading away. Ambrose Bierce's *Devil's Dictionary* definition of a boundary as "an imaginary line between two nations, separating the imaginary rights of one from the imaginary rights of another" seems more and more accurate.

In these unprecedented circumstances no individuals and no nations are acquiring sovereign power. Nor is it winding up in the hands of the corporate enterprises that are creating this brave new world. They are not quite as powerful as they seem, for even the strong among them may vanish from the scene at any moment, swallowed by another in a hostile takeover reminiscent of the way nations used to seize each other. And no corporation is without its own master: the billions of individuals and the many institutions who as consumers make the final decisions of the global marketplace. But even these consumers derive from their vast purchasing power no sovereign ability to shape the emerging global community. Their power is too amorphous, too scattered, too uncoordinated.

The institutions that may come closest to ruling globalization are the central banks, but they are totally independent of each other and each is jealous of its own national power, so their policies are not necessarily coordinated. And they, too, are hardly democratic. Their officials are not elected, and they meet in secret. The elected leaders of the nations who appoint them have ceded to them the responsibility to control inflation—and with it the capacity to stimulate or strangle employment and growth.

So forces generally responsible to no one, haphazardly moving across national boundaries and transcending traditional sovereign sensibilities, are transforming and homogenizing far-flung and once remote cultures, lives, and the spending and thinking habits of billions of people. No conscious force is shaping the new worldwide society—no sovereigns ruling by divine right, no sovereign nations, no sovereign individuals, no secret corporate conspiracy, no combination of these or other forces constitutes any kind of deliberate, thoughtful global decision-making process.

For many, the spread of capitalism through globalization has led to a significant improvement in living standards. All sorts of old and new products and services—some adding significantly to the quality of life, some rather less benign—have become available worldwide to everyone who can afford them. Profits, employment, wages, and consumer purchasing power have all risen for a great many of the world's people. It has been rudely discovered, however, that all this is very fragile. Those doing very well can suddenly suffer severe setbacks through no apparent fault of their own as an economic crisis in one country—like those suffered in Thailand and Russia in the '90s—can now cause immediate and painful convulsions in others near and far.

It is far worse for 3 billion people—half the human race. Uneducated, untrained, unemployed, unhealthy, ill fed, ill clad, ill housed, most of them are simply left out. They are struggling to survive on $2 or less a day while 250 individuals have accumulated more wealth than the 3 billion. The gap between thrivingly rich and miserably poor and bitter people and nations is not narrowing. It is widening dramatically in countless ways. There are the people who have become addicted to computers and cell phones, and there are the people—estimated to include half the human race—who have never spoken on a telephone. Despair and anger seethe and spread as the extremes of opportunity, opulence, and satiety are displayed on TV for all to see— except the many who've never seen even a village TV. But by word of mouth they, too, learn what they are missing.

If the essential needs of those whose deep and desperate plight is the unbearable reality of all their days and nights are ignored while market imperatives reign supreme, social upheaval will surely rise. Demands for drastic change will be made with increasing insistence. The global triumph of the free market over the planned economy after the collapse of Marxism may then prove to have been only a prelude to further sweeping change amidst mounting unrest and strife. Revolt against globalism and the governments of impoverished nations that go along with it willingly or unwillingly could then well come to match in violence that of the sovereignty struggles. "Beware the fury of the patient and long-suffering people," warns President K. R. Narayanan of India, the country with the most illiterate people, the most poor, the most malnourished. President Vaclav Havel of the Czech Republic cautions that "the voices of the people" must be heard and heeded, and that poverty "must be solved taking into account the human dimension, and not just the interests of investors." Bill Clinton, Tony Blair, and Nelson Mandela have warned that a "third way" must be found that takes people and profits into equal account and leads to a significant reduction in poverty. They pledged allegiance to a market economy but not to a market society.

Like pathfinders who have lost their way, however, these and other past and present leaders of nations have not yet managed to mark out the directions a third way should take. They seem to have some sort of a mixed economy vaguely in mind, but no agreement is in sight on how much regulation can be imposed on a market economy without undermining its capacity to generate the unprecedented prosperity it has brought to so many. Nor has any agreement been forged as to how decisions affecting the global economy should be made. There are compelling moral as well as practical reasons for hammering out such agreements. Three billion people cannot be forever condemned to an outer circle of despair in a world capable of offering them far greater opportunities. And Francis Fukuyama, the philosopher/political scientist whose commentaries one seems to encounter nowadays at every turn, admonishes, "The biotech revolution raises big moral issues that scream out for international governance and a common agreement on rules." He suggests that we don't want to just leave this to the market and have people designing babies in the Cayman Islands.

It's not as if efforts haven't been made to alleviate poverty while promoting growth, stability, and some degree of economic order in the world. As people and nations found themselves ever more connected with each other in the twentieth century, new international financial and economic institutions were created. The World Bank was to make loans to impoverished developing countries. The International Monetary Fund (IMF) was to operate like an international credit union, with nations making deposits in it and borrowing from it when need be. The World Trade Organization (WTO) was to work to eliminate trade barriers and to promote an open, equitable, and non-discriminatory trading system.

All three institutions proceeded to operate on the general assumption that "a rising tide lifts all boats"—that prosperity for some would mean prosperity for all. Rather soon complaints began to be heard. Corporations were awarded contracts to build dams and a vast array of other public works, and that did produce many jobs, but it was charged that too little emphasis was being placed on direct efforts to attack poverty, and that not enough attention was paid to protecting the rights of working men and women. There were also complaints that no notable attention was paid to protecting the environment and promoting a sustainable global economy. Quite recently *Business Week*, after duly noting the many benefits that the rise of market capitalism around the world has brought to so many people, declared in a special report, "The plain truth is that market liberalization by itself does not lift all boats, and in some cases, it has caused severe damage. What's more, there's no point denying that multi-nationals have contributed to labor, environmental, and human rights abuses."

The new institutions were originally given scant authority to really regulate anything. Rather, they were expected to advise and assist. The powers of persuasion of the World Bank and the IMF became immense, however, because they could grant or withhold such huge sums. Meanwhile, the rapid expansion of world trade—and all the problems that accompanied it—led in 1995 to a substantial increase in WTO's powers, including specifically the authority to impose sanctions upon nations and to invalidate any national laws found by WTO to be "in restraint of trade." This swiftly produced a brand new set of problems. Instead of being accused of doing too little, WTO was now accused of doing too much, and it compounded the aggravation by proceeding to exercise its new and unusual authority in an arbitrary and sometimes secretive manner. The sweeping nature of its decisions provoked angry controversy and drew vociferous protests that WTO was violating the sovereignty of nations. Environmentalists were outraged by WTO rulings that knocked down provisions of the US Clean Air Act and nullified laws designed to preserve rain forests and protect dolphins and sea turtles. Labor unions in developed countries were angered by WTO decisions that ignored the competition their members face from sweat shops, child labor, and workers in developing nations who have few if any benefits and no fair labor, minimum wage, and safety laws to protect them. Developing nations charged that WTO is dominated and manipulated by giant corporations and by the US and few other major developed nations that seek to protect their own jobs by promoting environmental laws and labor standards that would push up costs in emerging markets. Developed nations squabbled among themselves over such matters as what WTO should or should not do about such matters as farm subsidies, the exporting of hormone-treated beef, the labeling of genetically modified food, the banning of asbestos imports, and the outlawing of lead compounds.

These grievances culminated in the partly violent demonstrations in the streets of Seattle late in 1999 that prevented beleaguered delegates to a WTO summit session from negotiating a new global trade round or making any important decisions. Encouraged by that success, the protestors moved on to Washington for more protests and then to Prague where they failed in their attempts to totally disrupt the annual World Bank–IMF conference but did force a premature end to their deliberations. There was somewhat less violence than in Seattle, although a McDonalds, a Kentucky Fried Chicken, and a Dunkin' Donuts—all three seen as symbols of America's predominant role in globalization—were trashed in the heart of the Czech capital. The complaints about the behavior of the two leading institutions focused in good part on alleged Draconian austerity measures imposed on nations as conditions for loans, measures that would slash social services depended upon by many people who have little or no resources of their own, thus increasing rather than decreasing poverty.

That there is something to the protests is evidenced by the fact the Bank and the Fund together have loaned over $470 billion since they began their work a half century ago, yet half the people of the world are still mired in poverty. That they must do better has been acknowledged by the heads of both institutions. The president of the World Bank, James D. Wolfensohn, asserts that an underlying social structure must be developed that takes people and profits into equal account. Managing Director Horst Kohler of IMF says, "We are aware of huge unsolved problems. The most pressing of these is poverty which is becoming a major threat for political stability in the world . . . A global economy needs a global ethic." Director General Michael Moore of WTO chimes in saying it would be a mistake to ignore the con cerns of the protestors. "Those who oppose us are not fools and frauds," he admits. "We need to assert our leadership on these issues." Recognizing the legitimacy of concerns about the environment, he says, "There can be no doubting that in the last century this fragile earth has received a battering at the hands of mankind. We have polluted her air and water and soiled her landscape."

It was in part a failure to address issues of a similar nature that did much to end the first prospective global economy over a century ago. It had begun to develop in the mid 1800s, when great advances in transportation and communications—notably the steam engine, the telephone, the telegraph—created a boom in international trade and investment, just as the coming of intercontinental air travel, the computer, TV, and other modern creations are doing now. This first globalization was undermined by a protectionist backlash provoked by widespread fears of the effect cheap foreign goods and labor would have on living standards in the more developed countries. It was finally brought to an abrupt end by the outbreak of World War I, and then kept in abeyance by the worldwide depression and World War II. Thus decades went by before it got under way once again. If today's globalization is not to run the risk of succumbing like its predecessor to protectionism and to apprehensions about its impact on the quality of life generally, it is clear that these concerns will have to be dealt with.

But who or what can do so? Certainly the WTO, the IMF, and the World Bank, even with the best of intentions, cannot. They lack any such broad mandate, and their power and resources are limited. Certainly the UN as presently structured cannot, for it, too, has neither the mandate nor the power. And certainly the 192 separate and sovereign nations of the world have demonstrated no capacity to do so. They are the institutions that we depend upon the most for the regulation of human affairs, but their mounting plight has been summed up by Daniel Bell of Harvard in a few words that former Chancellor Helmut Schmidt of Germany is fond of quoting: "The nation-state is too big for the small problems and too small for the big problems."

This leads to a fundamental question: are the many institutions we have created in our efforts to achieve a reasonable degree of order and progress and a maximum degree of freedom adequate in view of the magnitude and complexity of the unprecedented problems we face?

A rising school of thought holds that they are not. One of its leaders is Dee Hock, the iconoclastic founder of Visa, a remarkably non-hierarchical business whose transactions are approaching two trillion dollars annually. Hock believes that we are in the midst of a global epidemic of institutional failure. Doubt and disillusionment about governments at all levels and the politicians and bureaucrats who are supposed to make them run is widespread, and must partly explain the sudden surge in the growth and influence of Non-Governmental Organizations. Many NGOs, like Amnesty International and Human Rights Watch, transcend borders and are global in their membership and reach. NGOs are now almost everywhere—in free and unfree nations, in such widely disparate countries as the US and Russia, Australia and Indonesia. In Bangladesh they are springing up so rapidly that there is no reliable count of their number and they, rather than duly elected local governments, now actually run more than half the nation's villages. Even authoritarian China has its own unique version of these institutions. There they are known as GONGOs—Government Organized Non-Government Organizations.

It is estimated that more Americans now do volunteer work in non-profit organizations than vote in national elections. Many of them devote substantial time—some full time—to their volunteer activities, compared to the few minutes it takes to vote. NGOs lack the democratic mandate that elections confer, and their success or failure is often measured by their ability to affect the actions of government, but Lester M. Salamon, Director of the Center for Civil Society at Johns Hopkins University, says: "There has been a general questioning of the capacity of the state to carry out a whole host of functions. This [NGO] sector represents another way of organizing the common business of society. I believe it is as important a development in the latter part of the twentieth century as the rise of the nation-state was at the end of the nineteenth century."

A similar consequence of the loss of confidence in governments and perhaps a sign of a loss of self-confidence within governments themselves lies in the steady growth in the use of referendums, with legislators turning to the voters and leaving it to them to make their own decisions at the polls on significant issues. There are now only six major democracies—Germany, Holland, India, Israel, Japan, and the US—that have never held a national referendum. In several countries, and in several US states, referendums have become—as the *Economist* recently put it—"a central feature of the political system." Voters in a number of nations and in many states of the US are turning to an even stronger instrument of direct democracy: initiatives. Initiatives enable citizens to decide issues all on their own by gathering signatures on petitions to place issues on the ballot, and then voting them up or down.

The basic principle at work here appears to be that individuals are taking unto themselves the sovereign right and responsibility to engage actively in influencing or actually making decisions on public matters that affect their lives.

This may be happening just in time. Immense disorder and worse can rise out of the weakness of nation-states if no workable way is found to solve global problems and to achieve global goals. Freedom and the forward march of democracy may be at mortal risk, with the processes of orderly self-government struggling to play a meaningful part in the sovereignty conflicts within and between nations and in the shaping of the emerging global community.

A crisis for all humanity may well be brewing in the cauldron of the common failure of separate sovereign nations to achieve a reasonable degree of justice and order in the world. Yet surely it is not ordained that we cannot succeed in doing so. Spreading chaos and violence need not be our certain destiny. There are other options.

Two great and significant experiments in the uses of sovereignty to contain conflict and improve the human lot are relevant. Both were undertaken in fairly recent history. One began two centuries ago in America and is still evolving. The other started half a century ago in Europe and is still unfolding.

Americans replaced a government that was over them with a government that was under them, according to Edward S. Morgan's succinct and simple explanation of the American Revolution and the creation of the United States. The founding fathers who were most influential in shaping the new country believed that sovereignty belongs to the people, not to any government. Thomas Jefferson wrote in the Declaration of Independence, "Governments are instituted among men, deriving their just powers from the consent of the governed." James Madison declared as he led the battle for the Bill of Rights, "All power is originally vested in, and consequently derived from the people." He stressed the need to interpose safeguards between the people and "the magistrate who exercised the sovereign power" to prevent encroachment on the sovereign rights of the people. Alexander Hamilton, who by no means intended that a new national government should be the sole possessor and proprietor of sovereignty in America, wrote in *The Federalist* that "a sovereignty over sovereigns . . . is subversive of the order and ends of civil polity."

This view was disputed by other early American heroes. Patrick Henry, the Virginia patriot who had stirred the emotions of the people with his eloquence and passion when he called for the American Revolution, complained bitterly because the first words of the proposed constitution were "We the people" instead of "We the states." He lamented Virginia's loss of the power of the purse and the might of the sword to a federal government that he viewed as foreign but that nonetheless was to be given the power to levy taxes and raise a standing army.

The prevailing majority at the Constitutional Convention brought about a limited transfer of sovereignty from the people and from the original thirteen separate and sovereign nation-states that were born after the Revolution to a new federal government: the United States of America. It had become clear that the Continental Congress, established when the vanquished British withdrew, was too weak and wasn't going to work. It had been given no power to write laws, only to issue what amounted to advisory opinions, and no executive or judicial authority had been established.

These incompetencies were cast aside in the new structure worked out at the Philadelphia Convention, but exactly how much authority should be granted to the proposed new federal government was fiercely debated and not fully determined. Votes were taken and decisions were ostensibly made, but a struggle for power between the separate states and the US government has been going on ever since—peacefully since the Civil War—and in the ebb and flow of history, elements of authority have moved back and forth between them. The Supreme Court is still grappling with the issue as it is repeatedly called upon to decide whether in this matter or that the President or Congress has encroached upon states' rights, or whether the states have sovereign immunity and are immune from suits charging that they have violated federal law.

It is very clear that when they formed a more perfect union, the founding fathers and the people they led by no means transferred all their individual sovereignty to the federal government. Part they kept in their own hands. Part had previously been lodged nearby in towns, cities, and counties. Part remained more distantly in the states. And only part was transferred still further away to the federal government.

The greatest experiment in the peaceful expanding and merging of sovereignty that has occurred since the creation of the US is now under way in Europe, the site and source of so many devastating wars over the centuries.

The historical suspicions, hatreds, and conflicting and colliding aims and ambitions that so deeply divided France, Germany, and other traditional European enemies far exceeded by any and every measure the differences and divisions between the thirteen nation-states that came together to form the American union. Yet these animosities have been thrust aside and war between the nations that have joined together in the European Union (EU) now seems unthinkable.

The EU started out in 1951 as a simple treaty signed by six nations to pool their coal and steel resources, but the man who inspired it, Jean Monnet of France, had a grander vision. "We are not forming coalitions between States," he said in 1952, "but union among people." And as Monnet expected, when the governments and the people of six nations found they could collaborate peacefully on coal and steel matters, they began to cooperate on broader concerns.

Other nations slowly joined the six—there are now fifteen—with many more aspiring for membership. Thirteen nations are officially recognized by the EU as candidates for membership, and negotiations are already under way with several of them. Nations must hold democratic elections, establish civilian control over the military, protect human rights, and pass other economic and political tests before they are admitted to membership.

The EU already has its own currency, the Euro; its own flag, a circle of twelve gold stars on a blue background; and its own anthem, Beethoven's *Ode to Joy*. Its citizens carry European passports and they can travel, reside, and work anywhere in the Union. Its elections are the first in all history held across long-established national frontiers.

In a feature unique in international institutions, delegates to the European Parliament are apportioned in general accordance with the population of the member states, rather than simply being allotted on the traditional basis of one delegate for each nation. Even more uniquely, the delegates are elected by the people of each country rather than appointed by their governments. These two provisions constitute a bow to the dawning concept that the sovereignty of half a billion European individuals is superior to the sovereignty of a few European nations. The first precedent for this was established when the principle of the primacy of the individual sovereignty of individuals was enshrined in the French constitution in 1958, replacing its 1791 provision that sovereignty "belongs to the Nation." The present constitution, drafted by General Charles De Gaulle, declares, "National sovereignty shall belong to the people who shall exercise it through their representatives and by means of referendum."

Disputes between the nations of Europe are marginalized in its Parliament as its members tend to sit with each other and vote with or against each other on the basis of their political affiliations and philosophies rather than on the basis of their nationalities. Their governments are forbidden to tell them how to vote. Thus German, French, and other members of leftist parties usually vote together on one side of an issue while German, French, and other members of rightist parties vote together on the other side.

The slowly expanding power of the originally quite weak Parliament was demonstrated in 1999 when an inquiry it had instigated into alleged corruption and cronyism in the more powerful European Commission led to the resignation of all twenty members of its Executive Committee. The Commissioners, who are nominated by their national governments but must be confirmed by EU's Parliament, are required to swear in their oath of office that they will never take orders from their governments. The Commission administers the laws of the Union and is the only body that can initiate legislation. Legislation can be enacted into law, however, only by action of both the Parliament and still another institution, the European Council. The Council is composed of the heads of government of the member nations who stand guard to protect the sovereign rights of their separate constituencies if the EU attempts to intervene in matters that lie beyond the realm of the authority granted to it. Important roles for nations are thus carefully preserved and protected, but an official EU document, *Europe in 10 Points*, states, "Member states relinquish a measure of sovereignty to independent institutions representing national and shared interests . . ."

As the member states gain confidence in EU institutions they cautiously expand their authority. At a summit meeting of the Commission late in 2000 a difficult and highly controversial revision of the number of seats on the Commission that will be allotted to national delegations as new members join EU was hammered out. The size of the delegations will be based on population but with smaller nations accorded extra seats to reduce the power of the larger. The Commission then voted to increase the category of issues that the Commission can decide by majority votes rather than by unanimous vote, thereby transferring the sovereignty of all member nations to the Commission insofar as the specified categories of issues are concerned. This expansion of the Commission's authority, however, is subject to ratification by the EU Parliament and by the parliaments of the member states. The Commission voted not to apply majority voting to certain categories such as taxation, social security, and immigration. On the delicate matter of monitoring the human rights record of members, it voted that an investigation can be launched only if one third of the member states vote to request it and nine tenths of the members approve.

The increasingly powerful European Court of Justice, the supreme legal authority for the EU, is often compared in its prestige and influence to the US Supreme Court, but it is distinguished from its American counterpart by one important practice intended to prevent charges that the justices cast their votes in accordance with pressures from the national governments that appoint them. Unlike the custom in the US, the opinions of the individual justices are never made public.

The rulings of the Court of Justice are leading to the development of a body of European law that presumably takes precedence over laws enacted by the EU's fifteen member states. This presumption is leading to legal challenges, analogous to those in the US between the federal government and the states, over the right of EU to overrule specific national laws.

Another judicial institution, the European Court of Human Rights, has a jurisdiction covering forty-one nations that have signed the European Convention on Human Rights. This court has a rapidly increasing workload that, according to Robert Liddell, a court spokesman, "reflects a growing consciousness of human rights and growing awareness that redress may be sought beyond the nation-state at the European level."

*Europe in 10 Points* states that two approaches, one federalist and one functionalist, provide the basis for the European integration that has hitherto been known only in the dreams of philosophers, visionaries—and Winston Churchill. The EU document declares: "Central to the federalist approach is the idea that local, regional, national, and European authorities should cooperate and complement each other. The functionalist approach, on the other hand, favors a gradual transfer of sovereignty from national to community level. Today, the two approaches have merged in a conviction that national and regional authorities need to be matched by independent, democratic European institutions with responsibility for those areas in which joint action is more effective than action by individual States."

A European foreign affairs structure, and a military command headquarters complete with forces of its own for peacemaking and peacekeeping missions, are supposed to be set up soon. A rapid-reaction force of as many as 60,000 troops is scheduled to be established. This would give the EU—some of whose members do not belong to NATO—the capacity to mount police actions without the participation of NATO and US forces.

A sense of shared responsibilities, as well as rights, appears to be slowly spreading among Europe's people. It is already a very different continent from the one that Henry Kissinger complained about not so long ago because "it didn't have a telephone." Key leaders of the EU's two most powerful continental nations, Germany and France, have sought to move toward a much stronger political and economic union. German Foreign Minister Joschka Fischer has called for the development of a European government on a federalist model with an elected president and a parliament with full executive and legislative powers. He has envisioned "a Europe of nation-states and a Europe of citizens." French President Jacques Chirac has urged Germany to join France in forming a core group that could move rapidly toward greater integration without being held back by nations that wish to proceed more slowly. Two former French presidents, Jacques Delores and Valéry Giscard d'Estaing, likewise have called for creating a more perfect union. Smaller states have expressed skepticism; a Finnish spokesperson, among others, has said Finland was not interested in unequal roles and structures.

Monnet, who started it all, was a quintessential Frenchman, proud of his country's unique characteristics and determined to preserve them. Yet not only did he lead the way to the creation of the EU and to France's membership in it, but he also saw it as a step along the way to some sort of world union. "The sovereign nations of the past can no longer solve the problems of the present," he said. "They cannot ensure their own progress or control their own future. And the European community itself is only a stage on the way to the organized world of tomorrow."

All is not sweetness and light in Europe, of course. The UK, Denmark, and Sweden still hold back from giving up the pound, krone, and krona, respectively, and joining in the troubled yet increasingly significant euro. France, Germany, and other members squabble over imports, immigration, and other sensitive matters. Small nations are fearful of being overwhelmed by the large and by the EU itself. Large nations want to reduce the role of small nations in EU decision-making. Tempers flair in nations that are told they must reform in fundamental ways before they will even be considered for membership in the club. Nations that are already members fret that admitting poor nations with no experience in democracy will undo EU cohesion and halt its progress. There are knotty questions about the status of Turkey and Ukraine. Tensions rise and questions abound when it comes to the matter of Russia. Will it become a member in some distant or not-so-distant day? Or will it become a foe undertaking to form its own rival Slavic federation—or something more menacing—out of the remnants of the Soviet empire?

Skeptics predict that nationalism will rise once again and the EU, managed in this scornful view by hack bureaucrats and incompetent politicians who have worn out their welcome in their native lands, will sink back into irrelevance. Despite many uncertainties and the fact that the Union is still a work in progress, however, among less pessimistic souls there is a new sense of vibrancy, of hope, of promise, of destiny, and a soaring vision of an ennobled Europe enjoying unprecedented peace and prosperity. These optimists foresee a Europe bringing—through the strict membership standards it imposes on those who wish to join it—new freedoms and opportunities to people to the South and East who have historically enjoyed precious little of either. They dream bold dreams of a Europe once again playing a leading role in the world not only economically—as it always has—but also socially, culturally, and intellectually in the tradition of the proud days of the Renaissance and the Enlightenment.

If it turns out that these are indeed the blessings that the great experiment in Europe yields, then a new and shining example will have been set of the profound advantages poolings of sovereignty can bring, a lesson for other regions and continents—and the world itself—to ponder and, perhaps, to heed.

Actually, the US and the EU are not the only examples of voluntary unions that have successfully enabled diverse people to live together in relative peace. The principle advanced by the Founding Fathers of the US that sovereignty belongs to individuals, not to nations, is now declared in the constitutions—if not always followed in the practices—of almost one hundred nations. The words used to state the principle vary from constitution to constitution and country to country, but typical of many is the language in the constitution of Greece, the country that experimented with democracy two thousand years ago. The Greek provision, almost identical to France's, states, "The sovereignty of the People is the foundation of Government . . . National sovereignty shall belong to the People who exercise it through their elected representatives and by way of referendum."

Switzerland is the most striking example of an enduring federation. It dates all the way back to 1291 when three separate cantons signed an "eternal alliance" that has survived through all the ensuing centuries. Switzerland is the harmonious home of four ethnic entities, four cultures, and four languages—French, German, Italian, and Romansh—and two religions, Catholic and Protestant. All of its diverse people share their sovereignty and their power with each other through a system of direct democracy that makes many of its decisions through initiatives and referendums. The authority of Swiss presidents is severely constrained, partly by a constitutional provision that limits them to one-year terms. The country now has twenty-three cantons and they are largely autonomous on matters of local concern. Switzerland has traditionally followed an independent, neutral, isolationist course in relationship to other nations. Its behavior during World War II when Hitler's troops arrived at its borders, and the way it dealt with refugees from the Nazi terror and the assets they deposited in the famous Swiss banks, has evoked widespread condemnation. Now it seems to be edging toward membership in the UN and the EU. Its dispatch of an armed military contingent to Kosovo on a peacekeeping mission was unprecedented in Swiss history.

All three nations on the North American continent, Canada and Mexico along with the US, are federations. Most of the countries of the world operate at least to some degree under principles that place at least some power below the national government in the hands of provincial, city, and other local officials. In many nations governors, mayors, and others are chosen in local elections, while in others where democracy is not yet in full flower they are appointed by the national government or by the ruling party. The spreading adoption of federal systems led to the recent convening in Ottawa, Canada, of the first global conference on federalism, attended by President Clinton and other heads of state and government who extolled the virtues of federal principles.

Experiments in new and advanced forms of organization and cooperation between nations are under way in other continents and regions. The Organization of American States promotes cooperation between the countries of North, Central, and South America, and a similar regional role has been undertaken by the Association of African States, the Arab League, the Asia Pacific Economic Cooperation group, and the Association of South East Asian Nations (ASEAN). The latter has found itself already facing circumstances analogous to those that confronted the original thirteen American nation-states in the loose confederation that preceded the union. When ASEAN was formed, its members agreed on one cardinal principle: there would be no interference in each other's sovereign internal affairs. Its members are now finding that certain affairs that they had considered internal are increasingly external in their ramifications and that non-interference is increasingly difficult to observe.

# CHAPTER 3

# The Sovereignty Revolution

## International Intervention

Are the lessons learned in America, Europe, and Switzerland, and being learned elsewhere, applicable to the world as a whole?

Certainly the differences among the people who inhabited the thirteen states when the Constitutional Convention met in 1787 were small compared to the differences among the people who inhabit almost 200 nations now. And certainly even the differences between the people of Europe that led to so many bloody conflicts over so many centuries are less than those among the people of the whole wide world. But great as the troubles were that led to the creation of the US and the EU, they were small compared to the troubles that cry out for global action today.

There was concern about the states surviving in any meaningful sense in the US and the EU even though the sovereign powers of the new unions were strictly limited. But they have survived for two centuries in America, survived so strongly that Professor Larry D. Kramer of New York University Law School recently wrote in the Columbia Law Review, "States do most of the governing in this country." Though it may be too early to finally tell at this stage, there is no evidence that the nations of Europe will not also survive.

The UN is the principal institution attempting to cope with the global problems that presently seem so intractable, but it lacks the requisite tools, and suggestions that it be given them are met with cries about national sovereignty and warnings about the doom of nations. History suggests, however, that nations are more likely to survive in the more orderly and stable world that they and their citizens could create by pooling a limited amount of their sovereignty than they are in the present anarchistic, lawless world of rising violence with the authority of nations waning and events spinning out of control as untamed forces work their will.

The instability and turmoil for nations that characterize their increasingly fragile existence in our disorderly world is reflected in a startling fact cited by Senator Moynihan in his remarkable book aptly entitled *Pandemonium*: only *eight* nation-states that existed in 1914 have not had their governments, and in many cases their borders, changed by violence since then. The eight are Australia, Canada, New Zealand, South Africa, Sweden, Switzerland, the UK, and the US. Ethnic quarrels and wars sparked by collisions over sovereignty fomented most of the violence in the rest. The average constitution is only twenty-two years old. Nations now are splitting and multiplying almost like amoebas. There were seventy-four nations at the end of World War II. There are now 192. There will soon be more. Mikhail Gorbachev, who saw his own floundering Soviet Union suddenly splintered into fifteen new nations, once remarked to me only half jokingly that there may be 800 nations tomorrow. Sergei Khrushchev, the historian son of Nikita Khrushchev, one of Gorbachev's predecessors at the helm of the Soviet Union, goes further. He notes that all told more than 5,000 sub-groups of humanity have identities and characteristics that could conceivably cause them to assert claims to sovereignty someday.

The dubious concern about putting national sovereignty in jeopardy that has deterred us from following globally the course chosen regionally in the US and the EU is having a totally unintended consequence. It is leading, in a perverse way, to the very withering away of national sovereignty that those possessed by the concern would avoid, as nations fail to control and even to influence and guide many world trends and events that impact the lives of everyone.

It is also putting our very lives in jeopardy. The first responsibility of the government of a nation is to protect its people from external threats, but it is ever more evident that today's national governments cannot be relied upon to fulfill this fundamental obligation. There have been 170 wars just since the end of World War II, killing an estimated 35 million people. Ninety percent of the victims were civilians. A century ago, the slaughter was far less: only 15 percent of the victims were civilians.

The forty wars raging today threaten the peace of the entire world, and the streams of refugees heading across borders in every direction to escape them offer devastating evidence that governments of many countries are failing to protect their citizens. There are at this moment 35 million refugees all told, many of them wandering helplessly about in their own countries, many seeking to escape the violence of governments that have turned in fratricide upon their own people. Gwin Prints of the Royal Institute of International Affairs in London estimates that in the twentieth century 140 million souls— many more than were killed in wars—perished "at the hand of their own pathological, totalitarian, authoritarian or communist governments." This ghastly toll began anew on January 1, 2000, as did the count of the victims of war.

Civilians living comfortably in even the most developed and seemingly stable countries should not be complacent. That includes those of us so fortunate as to live in the US, the most powerful and prosperous society the world has ever known. Our government is not about to turn on us any more than the governments of other tried and tested democracies are about to turn on their citizens. But no national government anywhere can be relied upon to protect its people, for at any moment any and all of us may be the victims of terrorists and their bombs or of an inadvertent and unintended US-Russian nuclear exchange that could pollute and poison the world.

It is not just in vital matters of war and peace that citizens cannot count upon their national governments for protection. If the widely expressed doubts over the sustainability of humanity's current economic, environmental, and social practices prove to be even half-way valid, other menacing global problems loom that threaten everyone. A seemingly classic and compelling example is global warming. The evidence mounts that the long-predicted warming is now beginning to occur. If, as is now generally believed likely, the warming is caused by the economic behavior of humanity, then the causes and cures are global and no nation can cope with it alone.

The governments and the people of most of the nations of the world do demonstrate their grave concern about these many problems and perils. Studies have been commissioned. Conferences have been held. Treaties have been written. Yet progress on most fronts has been limited. When it comes

to war and violence, many nations—with China and Russia notable dissent-
ers and France exhibiting considerable reluctance—are coming to the view
that it is necessary to disregard national sovereignty and to intervene *within*
nations like Iraq if they seek to acquire nuclear weapons, and that there is a
humanitarian obligation to intervene elsewhere if genocide breaks out or if a
nation simply collapses into total disorder.

There is, however, a small problem. There is no effective, reliable, and
generally acceptable way for the world community to decide where, whether,
and how to intervene and who should do it. No guiding principles or standards have been agreed upon. Sometimes decisions to intervene are made by
the UN, sometimes by NATO, sometimes by the US alone, and sometimes
despite extreme provocation there is no decision and no intervention. When
an intervention does occur it is on a selective and wholly undefined basis.
Interventions are likely when affairs get out of hand in a land in or near the
West, or if vital Western interests are threatened elsewhere. They are unlikely
in more remote places like Congo and Rwanda where even the most horrifying slaughters are deemed to have little direct impact in the West. Nor are
they to be expected in most circumstances if the intervening forces are likely
to suffer heavy casualties. No action is contemplated because of Russia's
brutal military actions in Chechnya or China's harsh repression in Tibet,
although what would happen if China invaded Taiwan is uncertain.

In military interventions that have occurred in recent years, the results
have been very mixed—witness Somalia, Lebanon, Iraq, Bosnia, Kosovo. US
forces have usually played the leading and sometimes the only role, with and
without UN and NATO approval and participation, but this predominant
role has not proven to be sustainable. Extreme caution has characterized the
US approach to intervention since a swooping raid into Somalia in 1993 by
an elite force of rangers on a mission that was supposed to take only an hour
suffered the loss of eighteen lives and seventy-five wounded in a long and
horrendous night. To add humiliating insult to bitter injury, the body of one
of the Americans was dragged through the streets of Mogadishu for all the
world to see on TV. Since then it has been US policy to intervene only when
swift success is virtually assured and when few if any American casualties are
likely. The preferred mode is to drop bombs from the safety of the skies and

to fire smart weapons from US ships at sea or planes located outside another state's territory. Nevertheless, the US still has the leading voice in international decision-making when interventions are contemplated, and this major US role is resented by others ranging from allies worried about their dependency on the US to those who fear the US seeks hegemony and intends to impose on the world a pax Americana. The US is accused of acting like a self-appointed global policeman and wry references are heard in international circles to something called "conditional sovereignty"—suggesting that a nation is sovereign only as long as its behavior is acceptable to the US.

The UN, created at the end of World War II "to save succeeding generations from the scourge of war"—those are the first words of its Charter—was supposed to solve these problems. But, like the League of Nations, created at the end of World War I for the same purpose, it was not provided with the tools to fulfill its mission. Neither institution was given a reliable source of operating funds or a peace or police force of its own. The decision-making processes of both were hamstrung by the veto. Every nation had a veto in the League. Five have it in the UN.

Should the UN be given the tools it needs?

To do so would require lodging in the UN a limited, carefully defined share of sovereignty, for without that no institution supposed to represent the people and nations of the world can be relied upon to function with adequate effectiveness.

This is not as revolutionary as it may sound. It is not a great departure from actions that have already been taken and that are occurring with increasing frequency.

Actually, most of the nations and people of the world have already placed a portion of their sovereignty in the UN. One hundred and eighty-two countries have taken this giant step, among them such major powers as Germany, Japan, and India. It is a sovereignty transfer that is strictly limited, applying only insofar as the nations are required to comply with Security Council decrees relating to order, security, and peace. "The members of the UN have agreed that the Council acts on their behalf," says Professor Henkin, "and they are legally committed to carry out its decisions."

The only nation-states that have not taken this step are two that have not joined the UN—Switzerland and the Vatican—and the five permanent members of the Security Council who possess the veto, China, France, Russia, the UK, and the US. Any of the five can exercise their sovereignty to block UN actions whenever they choose.

Each of the 182 nations has a seat, a voice, and a vote from time to time on the Security Council and thus can exercise its sovereignty there on a rotating basis. Ten members of the General Assembly are elected by it to sit on the Council for temporary two-year terms. It takes at least five votes from these temporary members for the council to adopt a resolution authorizing any action, for the Council can act only when a proposed measure is not vetoed by any of its five permanent members *and* is supported by a majority composed of at least nine of its fifteen members.

Portions of American sovereignty and that of other nations and their people have already been delegated to other regional and global institutions for a variety of purposes. It is seldom acknowledged and little recognized, but the fact is that this process has been slowly gathering momentum for more than a century as human relationships have become more and more interwoven and interdependent in our shrinking world. The earliest such actions had to do not with momentous issues like war, peace, and violence but with small and routine day-to-day cross-border commercial transactions and social intercourse. Prime early examples of treaties and institutions created for such purposes were the Postal Union, the Telegraph Union, and the Patent Convention, all negotiated in the latter half of the nineteenth century when the first signs and tokens of globalism were encountered. Each of these agreements brought about limited transfers of sovereign authority to global institutions. It had become clear that without these arrangements ordinary communications and business across frontiers would be needlessly difficult if not virtually impossible to carry on, and the development of international trade and commerce would be severely handicapped.

The terms of the agreements setting up these and like regimes and the delegation of powers to them to fulfill their purposes have the standing of international law. The US has joined over one hundred international organizations since 1945, and signed scores of treaties containing a clause providing that disputes over the meaning and interpretation of their terms shall be resolved by rulings of the International Court of Justice. However, compliance with the rulings of the organizations, with the provisions of the treaties establishing them, and with the rulings of the court depends not upon the traditional law enforcement infrastructure of courts, police, and prisons so familiar within nations but rather upon carrots, sticks, and self-interest. Those who violate the terms of treaties and conventions are unable to reap the benefits the system confers but instead suffer sanctions and other unpleasant consequences.

The most far-reaching and comprehensive system created thus far by the global community is the UN's 1982 Convention of the Law of the Sea. One hundred and thirty-three nations, including China, France, Russia, and the UK have formally signed and ratified it so far. The US is among twenty-five nations that have signed but not ratified. The nations that are fully aboard have agreed to participate in an ingenious process that offers alternative methods of mandatory conciliation of disputes, and to abide by the terms of whatever settlement the chosen method produces.

Article 137 of the Convention contains a unique provision that elevates sovereignty to a new and unprecedented level. It formally declares that in the open sea and everything beneath it all humanity is sovereign. The article states: "1. No state shall claim or exercise sovereignty or sovereign rights over any part of the Area or its resources, nor shall any state or natural or juridical person appropriate any part thereof. No such claim or exercise of sovereignty or sovereign rights nor such appropriation shall be recognized. 2. All rights in the resources of the Area are vested in mankind as a whole . . ."

Difficult and divisive issues arose during the drafting and signing stages of the Convention and plague it now in its ratification stage. Resembling the issues that swirl around the WTO, they involve economics and the environment and carry a vast potential for future controversy. The stakes are immense. Seas cover 70 percent of the earth's surface, and humanity's dependence upon them for food, minerals, and energy is bound to increase dramatically. The world has long accepted the concept of freedom of the surface of the seas for navigational purposes, but no similar tradition applies to the sea bottom, and all that exists between it and the surface. It remains to be seen whether resources there and rights to them wind up being developed and exploited by the most powerful corporations and nations or whether the principles of the sovereign rights of humanity set forth in Article 137 finally prevail.

The same sort of issues loom as the first ventures of our species into outer space commence and controversies, claims, and counterclaims arise over privileges, rights and regulations. Inestimable riches are to be reaped there, too, and the major matter of militarization of space has to be sorted out. If the US proceeds with its highly contentious plans to build a missile defense system, its advocates want to base surveillance and shoot-down components in space. China has warned that this "will turn outer space into a new weapon base and a battlefield." The US Space Command is indeed developing plans to base weapons in space. Other nations presumably have competing intentions. Still others want space demilitarized, with only "peaceful uses" allowed. They argue that space should have its own Article 137 proclaiming and protecting the sovereignty of all of us in the wild blue yonder.

When sending men to the moon as the first great advance into space began to seem within reach in the late '50s, the US military developed plans to transform the moon into a military base replete with guided missiles carrying nuclear warheads and with surveillance systems to spy on the Soviet Union. Before Neil Armstrong and Buzz Aldrin actually set foot on the moon on July 20, 1969, Congress enacted a law requiring that the first Americans to get there should plant the American flag, and this was duly done. However, in a display of remarkable restraint, Congress also declared, "This act is intended as a symbolic gesture of national pride . . . and it is not to be construed as a declaration of national appropriation by claim of sovereignty." Armstrong and Aldrin left on the moon beside the flag a plaque that bore these noble words, "We came in peace for all mankind."

Issues of sovereignty seem to arise almost automatically whenever representatives of national governments negotiate no matter what the subject. They also come up whenever government officials meet with experts and NGO activists and advocates at events like the UN Conference on the Environment and Development where a worldwide cooperative effort was launched at Rio in 1992 to grapple with such sensitive and complicated issues as global warming, sustainable development, and protection of endangered species. The UN sponsored a series of world summits on other burning issues in the 1990s. Their very titles are indicative of the array of serious priorities for the twenty-first century that have landed on the global agenda: The World Conference on Human Rights, the International Conference on Population and Development, the World Summit for Social Development, the Conference on Climate Change, the World Conference on Women, the City Summit.

At these sessions, thoughtful participants inevitably find themselves asking each other and themselves, "How do we solve these problems without getting into the matter of sovereignty?" They might well ask themselves, "What will become of the sovereignty of my nation—and all nations—if global problems simply get worse and worse because separate nations can't deal with them?"

It is when efforts are made to reduce violence and war within and between nations that the issue of sovereignty is encountered in its most intractable form. Yet that is also when the greatest modern changes in concepts of the sovereignty and inviolability of nations have occurred. This is particularly true when the subject is nuclear weapons and what to do about them.

The UN Charter was written before the atomic bomb came on the scene. If its authors had been aware of the bomb, perhaps they would have produced a stronger institution with a greater capacity to prevent further use of this mighty force. After the destruction of Hiroshima and Nagasaki, the US did propose that nuclear weapons be placed under control of the UN, but the USSR rejected this proposition and proceeded to acquire its own nuclear arsenal, and the costly and dangerous nuclear arms race was under way. Soon humanity was confronted by the Cuban missile crisis and a narrow escape from a nuclear Armageddon. A modicum of reason prevailed thereafter. The US and the Soviet Union agreed to put a cap on the size of their bloated nuclear arsenals in the first Strategic Arms Limitation Treaty (SALT). Mistrust was deep between the two nations, however, so to reduce the fears of each that the other might cheat, they began in SALT what led to a series of treaties that allowed unprecedented intrusions into their most sovereign and sensitive security affairs—intrusions that would have been unthinkable a few decades ago, but that are becoming commonplace in connection with verification of arms treaties.

New ground was broken in the first Strategic Arms Reduction Treaty (START), which went beyond the caps of SALT to commence verifiable reductions in Soviet and American nuclear arsenals. Other treaties allowing similar intrusions and dealing with chemical and biological weapons and land mines have been negotiated in recent years. These are intended to involve all nations, although they do not yet do so. Other treaties allow still more intrusions. One supposedly gives a mandate to the UN's International Atomic Energy Agency (IAEA) to examine nuclear facilities in every nation in the world except the five original nuclear powers—China, France, Russia, the US, and the UK—and the three states that later developed smaller arsenals, Israel, India, and Pakistan. Iraq is now creating what is likely to become a crisis by challenging the right of IAEA agents to inspect sites suspected of concealing efforts to produce nuclear weapons. Iraq's official explanation is that such inspections would violate the country's "national dignity and sovereignty."

The Comprehensive Test Ban Treaty (CTBT)—ratified by France, Russia, the United Kingdom, and a number of non-nuclear nations, but rejected in the first attempt to win approval in the US Senate, and not yet acted upon by China and a majority of nations—provides intrusive verification through warning systems to be erected and operated internationally on the sovereign territory of key nations. The regional Treaty on Conventional Forces in Europe places unprecedented limits on the size and composition of the armed forces of thirty nations, including Russia, authorizes on-site verification, and declares a conflict within a European nation is a legitimate concern of all European nations.

These and other treaties break the traditional ground rules against violation of national sovereignty in many ways, but they all share the same basic weakness that potentially or in reality limits the effectiveness and reliability of present international treaties and institutions. None of those that deal with highly significant and controversial affairs establish trustworthy systems that *require* nations to observe their terms. They do not contain provisions imposing penalties adequate to insure that a nation caught cheating will be compelled to comply. Thus is the sacred sovereignty of nations supposedly protected—but in fact jeopardized, since the absence of any effective mechanism to enforce the peace and to cope with other threats to humanity puts the safety, security, and survival of all nations and their people at serious risk.

Most treaties that are intended to commit all nations to agreements promoting peace look to the UN Security Council for enforcement. Yet due to the veto no nation can depend upon the UN for protection with any degree of certainty.

The frequent failures of the Security Council to act swiftly enough, or effectively enough, or even to act at all when armed combat, genocide, or ethnic cleansing breaks out somewhere—along with weaknesses the UN displays on other matters—are prompting a rising chorus of calls to strengthen its capacity to respond to crises and to fulfill other tasks assigned to it. There are many proposals that would give the UN new capabilities. A few of the less far reaching are beginning to win serious consideration, and could be agreed upon and accepted in some modified and modest form in the not too distant future. The time for others that are more fundamental and sweeping does not appear to be near at hand.

## Structural Change

And yet . . . and yet . . . the leaders and the people of Europe concluded after the calamity and horror of World War II that enough was enough, that they and their countries *had* to take drastic measures to end their constant and ever more destructive conflicts. Just so, the leaders and the people of the world are likely to be driven by the inexorable march of dangerous events to the realization that a fair and reasonable way *must* be found to make and implement global decisions not only in matters of war and peace but also on such issues as global warming, human rights, and the need for an economy that is both free and fair. And not just to redress global grievances and avert looming catastrophes, but to seize the vast opportunities and fulfill the highest hopes for the great advances in the human condition that science, technology, and the free economy are at long last bringing within reach. The day that realization dawns will be the day the restructuring of the UN—or, conceivably, its replacement by something better—lands on the human agenda.

The preferable and most logical approach would be to build on the foundation that has already been laid in the UN. All the world's nations except Switzerland and the Vatican are now members. It is slowly gaining strength and new responsibilities.

The more serious and carefully thought out proposals to reform and strengthen the UN and enhance its capabilities are all based on the shared experiences of humans the world over and on the fundamental principles of good governance that have developed over the centuries. They are applicable in one way or another to whatever body or bodies are created or chosen in an effort to bring greater freedom and order to a chaotic and violent world. It may be that fears of loss of individual and national sovereignty to one central global institution could stalemate efforts to endow the UN, or any other single institution, with enough sovereign power to make and carry out meaningful global decisions on the several fronts where they are called for. In that event, a number of separate and distinct world institutions may emerge as people and nations grope their way to a better managed world by transferring bits and pieces of their sovereignty to several different institutions, empowering them to cope with discrete issues and problems facing humanity. One institution could emerge to deal solely with the apparent common need to halt global warming, and perhaps also to take on other environmental threats to the quality if not to the actual survival of life on earth. Another could deal in a carefully limited but needed way with the economy and its many ramifications—the free market, trade, worker rights, poverty, sustainability, consumption. Still another could deal with weapons of mass destruction, perhaps under one regime, perhaps under three similar but separate institutions established to deal with each of the three categories, nuclear, biological, and chemical threats. Other global concerns could be dealt with in the same incremental and independent way. This is the way the judicial side of global governance seems to be developing. The International Court of Justice, created in 1946, has been slowly gathering respect and creating a body of law ever since, but its jurisdiction is limited, and now a drive is under way to supplement it with an international criminal court to "investigate and bring to justice individuals who commit the most serious crimes of concern to the international community, such as genocide, war crimes, and crimes against humanity."

In any event, whether the chosen instrument is the UN or not, the nature of principal suggested reforms is relevant as a new global architecture of governance emerges in whatever form it finally takes. The failures of the UN that are the consequence of its structural weaknesses offer lessons to be learned and applied, regardless of whether or not the UN becomes the major instrumentality of humanity's effort to do better.

The single most significant characteristic of any organization is how it makes decisions, how voting power is divided up among its members. There are exceptions, but in most international institutions each nation, no matter how large, small, strong, weak, has one vote. This is the formula in the UN. The allocation of one vote to each member nation in the General Assembly is supposed to represent the sovereign equality of states, but it is not as democratic and fair as it sounds. Monaco, a tiny principality with a population of 31,000 once described by Somerset Maugham as "a sunny spot for shady people" and best known for its Monte Carlo casino and its handiness for money laundering, has the same vote in the UN's General Assembly as China with its 1.3 billion people. Monaco and even smaller Nauru, population 11,000, can outvote China, India, the US, or any other large and powerful nation two to one. So can Monaco and Sudan, population 35 million, a wayward nation described not long ago by *The Wall Street Journal* as embodying "every evil that the UN was founded to fight: war, famine, genocide, dictatorship, religious persecution, human slavery, forced starvation, and repression of women."

It is obvious that the major powers are not likely to permit any meaningful grant of authority to the UN or any other international institution unless it is based upon a system of representation that takes the size and strength of nations, if not the nature of their governments, into account. It is in good part for that reason that they have only granted to the General Assembly the power to make recommendations. It cannot make binding decisions. It cannot legislate.

It won't, of course, be easy to change the one-vote-per-nation rule in the UN or to depart from it in new institutions. While large and powerful nations will oppose any proposal that would grant to the world's majority of small and weak nations the ability to make binding decisions that bind all nations, small and weak nations will resist any proposal that would do away with the cherished equal standing with the high and mighty nations that the one-vote-per-nation rule gives them. Yet unless a more realistic system of representation is devised, it will almost certainly be impossible to give any international institution the power needed to make decisions on behalf of the true interests of all nations, strong and weak alike.

A number of new approaches to representation have been proposed for the UN, and could apply as well to other institutions. One would accord votes in the General Assembly on the basis of the population of nations but with upper and lower limits. Nations with up to one million people could have one vote, for example. There could be a cap with all nations with 50 million people and more having, say, thirty votes, with a sliding scale for nations in between. Another approach would accord votes through a system of weighted representation that would allocate votes to nations on the basis of several factors—such as population, literacy, and productivity—the factors that already more or less determine the influence or lack of it that nations have in the world.

Yet another suggestion, known as the Binding Triad, would allow the General Assembly to enact legislation provided it was approved by majorities calculated on the basis of three different factors: first, the present one-nation-one-vote formula; second, population, with no nation allocated more than, say 15 percent of the total; and third, contributions to the UN budget, again with a cap. This approach would seem to protect the interests of both the strong and the weak alike. Under this approach, it would be exceedingly difficult to reach decisions and therefore far from easy to trespass upon the sovereignty of nations. Paul C. Szasz, a former legal advisor to the UN Secretariat, has commented that "because of the natural reluctance of most states to limit their own freedom and sovereignty, only the most urgent, essential and popular proposals would ever be adopted."

It was the pure, naked matter of preserving their own national sovereignty insofar as the UN was concerned that caused the five principal victors in World War II—China, France, the Soviet Union, the UK, and the US—to insist that they be given a veto over any and all actions and resolutions in the Security Council, a provision that has plagued the UN ever since its Charter was drafted in San Francisco in the heady days preceding Japan's surrender. The five were unwilling to permit the UN or any combination of nations acting through it to infringe upon their dominance and their freedom to act as they chose in the world.

There are many proposals now to revamp, strengthen, and democratize the Security Council, most of them designed to curtail the use of the veto. In present practice and in contrast to the frequent resort to the veto that occurred in the UN's early years, it is now rarely cast, but this is an informal development that is not due to any change in the rules. The power to veto is still there, and the fact that it can be used at any time to paralyze the Security Council dominates the dynamics of every controversial issue it takes up. One suggestion floating around the corridors of the UN calls for a formal agreement among the big five to refrain from resorting to the veto except when their "national interest" is clearly at stake. This mild first step might be followed in the course of time by amendment of the UN Charter to define and formally to limit the cases where the veto would be permitted. The outright abolition of the veto in some distant day is widely viewed as desirable, but that is a contentious matter of far greater complexity and magnitude, and it is not likely to occur until there is a fundamental revision of the system of representation in the Security Council as well as in the Assembly.

One reform that is supported by many nations including the US seems certain to be implemented in some form, perhaps reasonably soon. It would make the Council more representative of the world's people by adding a few nations to the privileged five that presently enjoy permanent membership. It is not proposed that the right to veto be extended to the new permanent members, and no consensus is yet in sight on who the new members should be. Germany and Japan are certain to be among the chosen. Brazil and Nigeria are prime candidates as the logical representatives of two unrepresented continents, Latin America and Africa, although the case for Nigeria is weakened by questions about its internal stability. India, second only to China in population and the world's largest democracy, is a leading contender, but her cause has been set back by a widespread sense that her recent contribution to nuclear proliferation by testing bombs should not appear to be rewarded any time soon with a seat on the Security Council.

A different proposal related to representation would change the way delegates to the UN are chosen. At present they are appointed by their national governments. It is suggested that instead they be popularly elected by the voters of each country. This is generally the way members of national parliamentary bodies are chosen the world over, and it's the approach that the EU turned to in order to reduce clashes caused by the differing interests of nations and to enable individuals to exercise their European sovereignty more directly.

Every list of ways to shore up the UN's overall capacity to function effectively stresses the need to put an end to its total lack of reliable and adequate financing for its assigned purposes. At present the UN is wholly dependent upon the payment of dues by its member nations—but sometimes they pay their dues on time and in full and sometimes they don't. The US was the worst offender at the turn of the century. It was over a billion dollars in arrears. This sharply undermines the UN's capacity to help keep the peace and to do as much as it might to help meet many human needs. One of the most serious consequences of that uncertain financing is that the UN's International Atomic Energy Agency's ability to conduct inspections to insure that no nation without nuclear bombs is secretly trying to make them is imperiled.

Professor James Tobin of New York University, the noted economist and Nobel Laureate, has proposed a solution that is gaining considerable attention and support as the UN's financial plight becomes increasingly apparent. The "Tobin Plan" would authorize the UN to receive a fee of one one-hundredth of one percent of international financial transactions. Consisting largely of speculations in currencies and commodities, these transactions now exceed a trillion dollars a day. The UN could receive more than one hundred million dollars a day from this single source. Other proposals that are certain to draw heavy opposition from obvious quarters suggest levies on military spending, arms sales, pollution, and other controversial activities.

An institution with major responsibilities for preventing global violence needs not only a reliable source of money but a reliable source of manpower personnel for whatever peace-keeping forces it has at its disposal. Yet here, too, the UN comes up short—with fatal consequences for millions of innocent people.

The UN has no peace-keeping forces at its disposal. When the Security Council authorizes an intervention in some troubled place, the UN General Secretary faces the difficult and sometimes futile task of pleading with nations to contribute troops for the mission out of their own armed forces. Sometimes nations respond, but sometimes they don't. The availability of adequate forces is usually uncertain, the timeliness of their availability is always dubious, and in any event command and control over them is a questionable proposition due to the unwillingness of the US and other major powers to permit their troops to serve under a UN commander.

When the slaughter began in Rwanda, UN Secretary-General Boutros-Ghali asked nineteen nations to contribute contingents from their armed forces to a UN peace force. He was turned down nineteen times. Result: 800,000 Rwandans were killed and the conflict spilled over into several neighboring countries in a struggle that still rages. Canadian General Romeo Dallaire, who was the commander of a lightly armed UN monitoring mission in Rwanda during the early stages of the genocide, has repeatedly stated that with 5,000 well-prepared soldiers he could have prevented most of the 800,000 deaths. An official UN investigation confirmed General Dallaire's judgment.

The UN's more recent unhappy experience in another African county, Sierra Leone, is a clear demonstration of the present predicament. In the spring of 2000, the Security Council authorized sending a force of 11,000 men into Sierra Leone to support a peace agreement that had failed to end a bloody civil war distinguished by a deliberate and ghastly terrorist policy of mass amputations and gang rapes of civilians employed by the rebel Revolutionary United Front. Of course, the UN had no force of 11,000 men nor any force of any size at all at its disposal. Secretary-General Kofi Annan proceeded to try to put such a force together, but the US and other major countries did not respond with any commitment of significant forces when he beseeched them to do so. The US did offer to help airlift troops in from other countries—an offer the UN turned down because it couldn't afford the price the US wanted to charge. The UK sent in paratroops ostensibly to evacuate British nationals from the country. They wound up fighting to stave off a sudden rebel assault intended to capture Freedom, the capital.

The UN was reduced to hastily patching together an ill-led force made up largely of ill-trained, ill-equipped, underpaid soldiers hailing primarily from impoverished Third World countries. The orders of its commander, who came from one country, were ignored by his deputy, who came from another. One contingent promptly got lost in the African bush, and more than 500 of its members were surrounded, captured, and held hostage by the rebels. Another contingent ran out of ammunition in the midst of a fire fight, and was compelled to flee. The British set out to train Sierra Leonean soldiers, but what that would lead to was unclear. The UK has attempted similar training exercises elsewhere, but according to the *Economist* many of the men they educate in the ways of war wind up using what they've been taught to mount coups, join rebels, or become bandits.

A proposed remedy that has come up every now and then ever since the UN was born, but at last may be on the verge of being taken seriously, would establish a standing peace force ready to strike swiftly when ordered into action by the Security Council to restore peace or halt atrocities. This force would not consist of contingents from the armed forces of nations. Instead a well-paid, well-trained volunteer UN force would be created to move in when eruptions of genocide, crimes against humanity, and general breakdowns of order occur amidst rising violence like the horrors that appalled the world in Bosnia and Rwanda.

Intervention by force of arms is not, of course, the best or only way the UN can attempt to deal with crises when nations go to war with each other or lose control of their own affairs. The UN strives to spot impending violence before it erupts and to prevent it by promoting dialogue and negotiations. It seeks to bring combatants together in peace talks if conflict breaks out. It promotes regional peacekeeping efforts. All these and other UN approaches to keeping the peace are severely hampered by the same financial weakness that hinders effective military interventions and harms UN operations generally. Adequate funds are sadly lacking to employ, train, and deploy skilled negotiators to hot spots, and to perform other missions that could save many lives.

Reforms along these general lines would transform the UN into a far more democratic and equitably constituted institution, and would thus open the way to lodging greater authority in it than seems possible under its present Charter. Perhaps other and better formulas will be devised and sooner or later adopted, but reforms will almost surely come in the course of time as the compelling need for limited, fair, and effective global decision-making and action becomes increasingly evident.

Whatever the course taken, whatever the choices made, issues of sovereignty will be front and center: sovereignty of individuals, sovereignty of nations, sovereignty beyond nations.

Centuries ago Copernicus taught humanity that the world is not the center of the universe. Now humanity is learning that the nation-state is not the center of the world. As the waning authority of nations becomes clear and the fact that national sovereignty is not the be-all and end-all of sovereignty, apparent questions about citizenship are inevitably arising. *U.S. News and World Report* recently observed, "How citizenship will fare in an age of weakening nation-states—so far the strongest protectors of the rights and liberties of citizens—is one of the great questions of our time."

When a nation becomes the violator rather than the protector of the rights and liberties of its citizens, it is now often the UN that is called upon by the conscience of humanity to intervene. When it becomes apparent that a global problem is beyond the capacity of nation-states to resolve, it is the UN that is increasingly looked to for action. So the answer to the *U.S. News* question will likely be found to lie in adding one more layer of citizenship—world citizenship—to the national and lesser layers among which sovereignty is presently dispersed. This would at long last enable individuals to act upon and embrace not only their traditional national citizenship, patriotism, and allegiance, but also their global citizenship, their planetary patriotism, their allegiance to humanity.

Many Americans already think of themselves in that light. A recent survey conducted for the Center on Policy Attitudes found that 75 percent of Americans agree with this statement: "I regard myself as a citizen of the world as well as a citizen of the United States." Ronald Reagan, about as American as they come, used almost the same words when he addressed the UN in 1982, saying, "I speak today as a citizen of the United States and of the world."

The looming task is evident. It is to carry forward in the world the work that was first undertaken in Switzerland so long ago, in America more recently, is now well launched in Europe, and may also be faintly found in its first dim glimmerings in the regional efforts to cooperate transnationally in other countries and on other continents.

If no giants appear to lead the way on this path already marked out and partially traversed, then it will fall to the members of civil society to demand more of the leaders they have—if need be engaging in a supreme exercise of their own sovereignty by transforming leaders into followers who are made to understand that common people will accept nothing less than uncommon actions from them.

The prospects for humanity would be considerably brighter if, looking to the lessons of history for guidance, we were to set out consciously and deliberately to build a world community based upon democratic principles, upon the rights and responsibilities of its citizens, and upon the exercise of their individual sovereignty under the rule of law.

No better way has been found to make and implement decisions in nations and in the communities within them.

No better way has been suggested to make and implement decisions globally.

History reveals no other way consistent with liberty to reduce chaos and conflict and to replace it with a reasonable and reliable way of conducting human affairs.

It is the only alternative that we humans have found to the savage disorder of anarchy or the stifling order of authoritarianism.

The principle that the deliberate pooling, through democratic processes of consent, of strictly limited and carefully defined portions of the sovereignty of individuals so as to obtain what cannot otherwise be had is the basic operational principle of free and lawful human society.

This seems to be as fixed and inexorable a law of human nature as the physical laws of gravity or thermodynamics or relativity—or of what components must be assembled just right to create the sort of nuclear explosions that lurk in our future if we fail to master our fate.

# PART II

# Responsive Essays

# Hazards, Choices, and Hope

JANE GOODALL

Alan Cranston's treatise on sovereignty, which he completed just before he died, and just before the world came crashing into the twenty-first century with the fall of the World Trade Center, is eerily predictive of the conflict that has since consumed the world. Alan all but spelled out how Osama Bin Laden would bring his war of terror directly to the territory of the United States. He saw clearly the dangers that were lurking, and I shudder to think that his foresight may continue to prove accurate. I find the following paragraph from his essay to be most unsettling:

> The creation of nuclear weapons and their proliferation into many hands is the most ominous fact that emerged from the unflowered carnage and unforgotten sorrow entombed with the remains of the twentieth century. It separates today and all the tomorrows from all the yesterdays. Wars once had their limits. Despite whatever horrors humans experienced through the centuries, they have always been able to say, "Life goes on." That may no longer be an accurate assessment of the human condition.

Alan (everyone who knew him called him Alan) spent most of his time and energy working to alert the world to the horrific dangers posed by nuclear weapons. Occasionally I had the privilege of working with him, and I continue to work with the Global Security Institute, an organization he founded that works for the ultimate goal of eliminating all nuclear weapons. It is a great honour to be able to contribute, even in a small way, to his final effort to provide an alternate, hopeful vision for the future of the world.

Alan died before the terrible attacks of September 11 but, as mentioned, he had predicted such incidents, and he had already identified the roots of the conflict we are now caught up in. The "war" on terrorism that was declared following 9/11 and the ensuing global conflict, in which we are now ensnared, is a war that Alan believed was, in large part, a war about sovereignty. Let me quote Alan's comments onthe first attack on the World Trade Center in 1993.

> The bombing of the World Trade Center in New York was a direct and ominous import into our country of the terrorism creating so much havoc elsewhere, carried out by militant and fanatic Islamic fundamentalists in retaliation for various perceived grievances including our intervention in the sovereignty struggles of the Middle East. Its toll was six dead, 1,000 injured. There are dark warnings of worse to come as terrorists proclaim they will wage a holy war against the United States and its citizens wherever they may be as long as we keep our "infidel" forces in Islamic lands in what they view as irreverent violation of their sacrosanct sovereignty by the "Great Satan."

Yes, Alan saw the writing on the wall and we are going through what may well be the most frightening period in human history to date, for never have the weapons of "conventional" war, such as those unleashed by the United States against Iraq, been so deadly, so powerful—or so costly. It seems very clear that we have the capacity to destroy life on earth, as we know it. Yet at the same time the human brain has created technology that has hugely benefited people around the globe. It has enabled us to walk on the moon, communicate through e-mail and the Internet, to cure diseases that would have killed us a few years ago. Unfortunately scientific ingenuity has also conceived weapons of mass destruction—and the threat posed by biological, chemical, and most frightening of all, nuclear weapons is real and immediate. How did we get into this sorry state of affairs? Is our capacity to destroy ourselves a uniquely human phenomenon, or is it something we have inherited from our stone-age ancestors? I have studied the behaviour of chimpanzees, our closest living relatives, for over forty years and this study has yielded some information about the origins of good and evil, and the origins of warfare, that may be of more than academic interest as we strive to understand our current predicament.

### The Roots of Evil

Louis Leakey sent me to Gombe with the hope that a better understanding of chimpanzee behaviour might provide us with a window on our past.

He was right. The study of the chimpanzees of Gombe that began in 1960, and data from studies of chimpanzees in other parts of Africa and in captivity, has helped us understand a great deal about our own nature, about how we got to be the way we are. In particular, it helps us to understand the evolution of human aggression.

Louis, farsighted genius that he was, told me he thought my work would take at least ten years to complete, and this at a time when just one year for such a study was almost unheard of. Of course, when I first stepped foot on the sandy beaches of Gombe on the shore of Lake Tanganyika, I had no plan to remain there for ten years. Yet had I stopped after only ten years, I should have continued to believe that chimpanzees, though very like us in behaviour, were rather *nicer*. Then came a series of shocking and horrific events.

In 1971 one of our researchers observed a brutal attack on a female of a neighbouring chimpanzee community. She was set upon by a group of "our" males who hit her and stamped on her, one after the other. During the course of the assault, which lasted more than five minutes, her infant of about eighteen months was seized, killed, and partially eaten. The mother managed to escape, but she was bleeding heavily and was so badly wounded that she probably died later.

We discussed the attack back at our research station late into the night, and decided it must have been a bizarre, once-only aberration. After all, the ringleader, Humphrey, was the alpha male and most of us considered him to be somewhat of a psychopath with a history of vicious attacks on females of his own community. Humphrey, we felt, must have encouraged the other males to behave in a way that seemed, at the time, to be so uncharacteristic. But, sadly, my picture of the "noble ape" was just as mythical as the "noble savage"—we would witness many more incidents of brutal inter-community aggression, several of which led to the killing of the infants of the female victims.

By 1974 it was clear that the once peaceful-seeming chimpanzees were heavily engaged in what amounted to a sort of primitive warfare. This had begun when the chimpanzee community, whose members I had known so well, began to divide. Seven adult males and three mothers and their offspring began spending longer and longer periods of time in the southern part of the range over which the whole community roamed. By 1972 it was obvious that these chimpanzees had formed an entirely new and separate community. The southern, "Kahama" community (as we had named it) had given up the northern part of the range, while the Kasakela community now found itself excluded from places in the south where it had previously roamed at will. When males of the two communities encountered one another in the overlapping zone between the two, they threatened one another; the group with fewer males gave up quickly and retreated into the heart of its home range. This was typical of the territorial behaviour shown by many species of mammals and birds.

But suddenly the aggression became more serious. The first deadly attack was seen by our senior field assistant, Hilali Matama. Six Kasakela males moved silently toward their southern border where they encountered one of the young Kahama males, Godi, feeding quietly by himself. When he saw them he tried to flee, but was seized and held to the ground while the Kasakela thugs beat him up for ten minutes. Then they left him lying on the ground, screaming weakly. Slowly he got up, still screaming, and gazed after them. He must have died of his wounds, for he was never seen again.

That was the first of a series of brutal assaults perpetrated by the powerful Kasakela community on individuals of the breakaway community: the Four-Year War. And it was not only adult males who were victimized, but the adult females also. All the attacks lasted between ten and twenty minutes and resulted in the subsequent death of the victim. All told, four of the seven breakaway males were seen to be attacked and a fifth was found dead, his body mutilated in a way that indicated he had also been victimized by the Kasakela males. The other two simply disappeared. One of the three adult females of the Kahama community was subjected to a horrific attack and died of her wounds; the other two vanished. In other words, during the war, the entire community that moved south was annihilated—with the exception of three young childless females. The victorious males actively recruited them.

The four years from 1974 to 1977 were the darkest in Gombe's history, and some of the most intellectually and emotionally challenging years of my life. Our peaceful and idyllic world, our little paradise, had been turned upside-down: The Four-Year War was devastating, but it was not the only violence that overtook our community. Two adult female chimpanzees began killing and eating the infants of others within their own group; the cannibalism stopped only when the two perpetrators finally gave birth to infants of their own. And the violence of human conflicts spilled over into our world as well, with the high-profile kidnapping of four of my students who were held for a ransom that was paid—and then helped to finance a civil war in Congo-Zaire that led, years later, to the overthrow of President Mbutu.

All my life I had known about kidnapping and ransom, and even experiencing it firsthand did little to change my view of the dark side of humanity. However, the brutal killings observed among the chimpanzees were different: they changed forever my view of chimpanzee nature. Suddenly, I had found that chimpanzees could be brutal—that they, like us, had a dark side to their nature.

For months I struggled to come to terms with this new knowledge. Often I awoke at night with horrific pictures of violence in my mind, of adult chimpanzees, their lips smeared with the blood of another; twisting and breaking the bones of a victim; of Madam Bee lying hidden under the vegetation, slowly dying of her terrible wounds, while her ten-year-old daughter tried to comfort her, gently grooming her and keeping the flies away.

When I published the first observations of inter-community killing at Gombe I came in for a good deal of criticism from certain scientists. They told me that these data would enable irresponsible scientists and writers to "prove" that our human tendency to engage in conflict is innate, that war is, therefore, inevitable—an unfortunate and regrettable legacy from our brutal ape-like ancestors. It was my first experience with the politics of science, the pressure to publish or not to publish for political, religious, or social reasons.

It was during the early 1970s that the subject of aggression became so highly political. This was hardly surprising, since questions about the nature of aggression were still linked with the horrors of the Second World War that we had recently lived through. On one side of the debate were those who maintained that aggression was innate, coded in our genes; on the other, those who believed that a human infant came into the world like a blank sheet of paper upon which the events that occurred during childhood would be etched and would determine all subsequent behaviour. One ethologist, whom I had always greatly admired, came out strongly on the "blank slate" side of the controversy. I shall never forget asking him, over a cup of coffee: "Do you *really* believe that all aggression is learned? I don't see how you can, as one who studies animal behaviour." "Jane," he replied, "I'd rather not talk about what I really believe." He went down in my estimation.

I had gone to Gombe neither to prove that the chimps were better or worse than humans, nor to provide myself with a platform for making sweeping pronouncements about the "true" nature of the human species. I had gone to learn, to observe, and to record what I observed; and I wanted to share my observations and reflections with others as honestly and clearly as I could. Certainly I felt strongly it was better to face up to the facts, however unsettling, than to live in a state of denial.

I concluded back then, and I still believe, that it is pointless to deny that we humans harbour innate aggressive and violent tendencies. The quite irrational surges of anger I felt as a mother when my own precious infant seemed to be threatened are proof enough for me. Many scientific experiments have shown that aggressive patterns are, at the very least, easy to learn. In the early 1970s, when I was an associate professor at Stanford, the psychiatrist Robert Bindora was conducting an experiment to test how readily small children learned aggressive patterns. He produced a dummy human figure, set it in front of a group of kids between two and three years old, then proceeded to beat, pummel, punch, stamp on, and kick it. He repeated each of these actions several times, slowly and clearly. Then, at varying times afterwards, he gave these same children access to the dummy and recorded their response. As might be expected, his little subjects eagerly attacked the figure, performing many of the same actions that he had demonstrated. A good argument against allowing small children to watch violence on television. (I begged for a similar experiment in which the dummy would be kissed, embraced, stroked, and so on. But to the best of my knowledge this was never done.)

The aggressive behaviour of the Gombe chimpanzees provided fuel for much theorising. But while other scientists were eagerly using this Gombe data to substantiate or refute their own pet theories on the nature of *human* aggression, I was trying to understand a little better the nature of *chimpanzee* aggression. My question was: How far along our human path, which has led to hatred and evil and full-scale war, have chimpanzees travelled?

## Precursors to War

It is both fascinating and appalling to learn that chimpanzees are capable of hostile and territorial behaviour that is not unlike certain forms of primitive human warfare. War had always seemed to me to be a purely human behaviour. Accounts of warlike behaviour date back to the very first written records of human history; it seems to be an almost universal characteristic of human groups. Wars have been fought over a wide range of issues, including culturally and intellectually determined ideological ones. They have functioned, at least ecologically, to secure living space and adequate resources for the victors. To some extent too, they have served to reduce population levels, thus conserving natural resources.

It has actually been suggested that warfare may have been the principal evolutionary pressure that created the huge gap between the human brain and that of our closest living relatives, the anthropoid apes. Whole groups of hominids with inferior brains could not win wars and were therefore exterminated.

When we think of war, we usually picture vast armies on the move, terrifying confrontations between men mounted on horses, marching on foot, driving armoured jeeps and tanks, flying fighter planes or bombers, and, in the worst scenario, pressing buttons that, in an instant, could destroy whole countries. Human wars are waged between countries; and between factions within countries—revolutions and civil wars have been among the most brutal of all.

Whilst warfare in its typical human form is a cultural development, certain pre-adaptations must have existed in our earliest ancestors to permit its emergence in the first place. Do we see evidence of such tendencies in chimpanzees? Certainly they are aggressively territorial. Not only do they protect their home range from incursion by "strangers"—that is, individuals of either sex (with the exception of adolescent females) from neighbouring communities—but they also actively patrol the boundaries of their home range at least once a week, monitoring the movements of their neighbours. And not only do they *defend* their territory; they also sometimes *enlarge* it at the expense of a weaker neighbour.

One of the most significant facts established about human behaviour, as it relates to warfare and other acts of violence against conspecifics, is this— cultural evolution permits the development of *pseudospeciation*. Pseudo-speciation, or cultural speciation as I prefer to call it, means among other things that the members of one group (the *in*-group) may not only see themselves as different from members of another group (the *out*-group), but also behave in different ways to group and non-group individuals. In its extreme form, cultural speciation leads to the dehumanizing of out-group members, so that they may come to be regarded almost as members of a different species. This frees group members from the inhibitions and social sanctions that operate within the group, and enables them to direct acts toward "those others" which would not be tolerated within the group. Slavery and torture at one end of the scale, ridicule and ostracism at the other.

Unfortunately, cultural speciation has become very highly developed in human societies around the world. Our tendency to form select in-groups from which we exclude those who do not share our ethnic background, socio-economic position, political persuasions, religious beliefs, and so on, is one of the major causes of war, rioting, gang violence, and other kinds of conflict. We find examples of our human tendency to form in-groups from which we exclude others in our cities, towns, and villages, in schools and neighbourhoods. Children very quickly form exclusive groups, sticking together, supporting each other, and distancing themselves from all others. Children who have formed such a group can be extremely cruel to "outsiders" and some children suffer intensely as a result. Today, cultural speciation is obvious in the terrifying evolution of the modern gangs. Gangs similar to Los Angeles's Crips and Bloods exist throughout the world with their identifying colours and graffiti and other cultural differentiations. There are countless other examples.

In the late 1970s, as I tried to understand the relationship between chimpanzee aggression and human violence, there was much evidence of the evils of in- and out-grouping among human peoples around the world. There were the ethnic, political, and religious hatreds in Rwanda, Burundi, Israel, Palestine, Cambodia, Northern Ireland, Angola, and Somalia. Genocide, or *ethnic cleansing*, had led to the killing of hundreds and thousands—nay, millions—of humans.

It is particularly shocking to reflect on the extent to which different religious groups have, from the beginning, tried to force their beliefs on others. The number of wars throughout history that have been fought over religious issues is staggering. The so-called holy wars—fighting over whose god was *the* God—resulted in an incomprehensible amount of suffering inflicted on unbelievers by those who had the upper hand at the time.

Clearly cultural speciation has been crippling to human moral and spiritual growth. It has hindered freedom of thought, limited our thinking, and imprisoned us in the cultures into which we were born. And, provided we remain locked within these cultural mind prisons, all our fine ideas about the Family of Man, the Global Village, and the uniting of nations, are just rhetoric. (Although I suppose there is some comfort in knowing that at least we realise how we *ought* to want to live, and the kinds of relationships we *ought* to want to have!) But unless we "walk the talk," racism, bigotry, and fanaticism, as well as hatred, arrogance, and bullying, will continue to flourish. Cultural speciation is a barrier to world peace. So long as we continue to attach more importance to our own narrow group membership than to the "global village" we shall propagate prejudice and ignorance.

My chimpanzee studies have persuaded me that the dark and evil side of human nature is indeed deeply rooted in our ancient past. We have strong predispositions to act aggressively in certain kinds of contexts; and they are the same contexts—jealousy, competition for food or sex or territory, fear, revenge, and so on—that trigger aggression in chimpanzees. Moreover, they show similar postures and gestures to ours when they are angry—swaggering, scowling, hitting, punching, kicking, biting, scratching, pulling out hair, chasing. They throw rocks at each other. Without a doubt, if chimpanzees had guns and knives and knew how to handle them, they would use them.

In some respects, however, human aggressive behaviour is unique. Thus while it seems that chimpanzees have *some* awareness of the pain they inflict on their victims, they are surely not capable of cruelty in the human sense.

Only we humans inflict physical or mental pain on living creatures *deliberately* despite—even *because of*—our knowledge of the suffering involved. Only we, I believe, are capable of evil. And in our evilness we have designed a variety of tortures that have, over the centuries, caused unbelievable agony to millions of living, breathing human beings. Human wickedness is immeasurably worse than the worst aggression of the chimpanzees.

But does that mean that we humans must be forever enslaved to our evil genes? Surely not. Surely we, more than any other creatures, are able, if we so wish, to control our biological nature? And while it may be true that aggressive tendencies are part of our genetic inheritance, so too are characteristics of love, compassion, and altruism. Chimpanzees show far more caring, compassionate, and altruistic behaviour than brutal, aggressive behaviour. And even as we humans are capable of acts of aggression that are far worse than anything chimpanzees are capable of, so too are we capable of heights of altruism that are denied to chimpanzees with their less sophisticated intellects. A chimpanzee, seeing a companion in trouble, may rush to the rescue. Indeed, individuals have risked and even lost their lives in trying to save drowning companions. But such an act of self-sacrifice is an instant response to seeing another in trouble. Humans respond, instinctively, in the same way. But we will also risk our lives—or our reputations—in "cold blood," as it were. We may decide to help another even after thinking through all that we may have to suffer, as a result, at a future date. There are innumerable examples of this kind of altruism in war.

## On Sovereignty

Not only do we have the ability to nurture or destroy, but we also have the ability to be aware of our actions and thus make choices. Unavoidably, this blessing or burden makes us responsible for our actions.

Humans have the unique capacity to consciously and intentionally organize institutions to control our behaviour and thus we create laws and political institutions to externalize controls over our own actions and govern our choices. This capacity for self-governance might be the necessary balance to our destructive abilities.

We are capable of extending our aggressive capacities to levels of violence that can destroy us. We are also capable of being negligent in controlling ourselves when our greed to dominate nature and harvest its resources outstrips its capacity to replenish. Unsustainable methods of providing livelihoods, and nuclear weapons, are examples of activities that beg for control. Moreover these issues are global in nature. There is presently an unwillingness on the part of nations to find organizational structures that will allow our sense of reason to curtail these dangers sufficiently. The idea of limiting power is repugnant to leaders of some governments. Yet it is clearly necessary; we might be in a race against time to solve this institutional problem.

Alan's approach to sovereignty forces us to rethink the challenge and places the issue squarely on the shoulders of the individual, exactly where it belongs. It is both awesome and empowering to be reminded that you and I are ultimately responsible for the welfare of the whole, and that we are the foundation of sovereignty and thus responsible to work to better the world. That is how Alan Cranston lived and that is what his book calls us to achieve, a higher sense and ability to be globally responsible.

### Reason for Hope

The question I am asked most often as I travel around the world springs from people's deepest fear: "Jane, do you think there is hope?" Is there hope for the rainforests? For the chimpanzees? For the people of our planet, rich and poor alike? For the planet itself, our beautiful planet that we are spoiling? Is there hope for us and for our children and grandchildren?

Sometimes it is hard to be optimistic, for we are, indeed, destroying our planet. The affluent societies around the world, with their unsustainable life styles, are continually draining the last natural resources from mother earth. In many parts of the developing world people are living in desperate poverty. When more people live on an area of land than it can support, and when they cannot afford to buy food from elsewhere, they increasingly destroy their environment. International agro-business is forcing more and more peasant farmers into the misery of overcrowded cities. The forests are going, the soil is eroding, the water tables are drying, the deserts are spreading.

Droughts and floods are getting worse. In so many places there is a vicious cycle of hunger, disease, poverty, and ignorance. Everywhere we see human cruelty, greed, jealousy, vindictiveness, and corruption. In our big cities we see crime, drugs, gang violence; and thousands who are homeless, their few belongings in prams or grocery carts or on their backs, living, sleeping, and dying on landfills, in doorways, on gratings. There are ever growing numbers of street children. There are ethnic conflicts, massacres, and broken peace treaties. Millions of people have been killed or maimed with bullets, machetes, and land mines. Millions more have become refugees. There is organised crime, sale of arms; and an international black market in nuclear materials from Russia's vast and crumbling nuclear arsenal. International terrorism, even before 9/11, developed a new and more sinister face—and the continued, ominous, almost forgotten threat of global terror, wielded in the form of the nuclear weapons of the United States and the other nuclear countries, plays a monstrous and unforgivable role in keeping us locked in this terrible situation.

Throughout the world Americans and their allies are, increasingly, looking over their shoulders, fearful not of their own shadows but those thrown by their own countries. Terrorism, with its suicide bombings, is fuelled by pure hate, by fanatical hate—that is learned, that is taught. And, as Alan says, much of this hatred is sparked by Arab anger at the interference of America in the way they govern their states, by America's support of Israel, and by America's blatant tactics designed to give her dominion over the world's oil fields.

All this would seem to suggest a hope-less millennium ahead. It is as though we are on a large ship. The lookout in the bow suddenly sees rocks ahead and alerts the crew. Yet it takes time for the big vessel to change course, so all attempts to avert disaster will fail and there will be a shipwreck. Of course, it will take time for the ship to disintegrate in the waves. Our world will end "not with a bang but a whimper." It is easy to imagine that such a fate awaits life, as we know it, on Spaceship Earth.

Remember Alan said the time might come when we would no longer be able to say, after some horrifying experience, "Life goes on."

Yet despite this, I do have hope for the future. The vast number of people around the globe who protested the bombing of Iraq suggests that individuals truly are beginning to believe that their actions will make a difference, even if they are facing up to the giant super-power that is the United States of America and the unprecedented might of its war machine with its obscenely huge budget. The protests against the dark side of globalisation, the huge power of the international multinationals, are getting ever better attended and better organised. Citizens are becoming increasingly determined to have a voice in the decision making process. More and more people realise that we need change in many areas of our lives, and that these changes must be made by us, the people. If we go on leaving it to others, shipwreck is inevitable.

Alan and I were united in our belief that individuals, working together, have the power to effect change and that, by taking informed and compassionate action, we can make this world a better place for humans, animals, and the environment.

Jane Goodall PhD, DBE
Founder, Jane Goodall Institute
UN Messenger of Peace
17 April 2003

# Sovereignty and Duty

JONATHAN GRANOFF

S enator Alan Cranston gifted us with *The Sovereignty Revolution* because of his profound love.

I recall Alan once pondering that this planet might be the only place in the universe where the capacity to love exists. Couple that insight with a life lived in the crucible of political service and historical conflict and it is natural that his gift would be filled with wisdom. Although one might emphasize different particular countries and conflicts today, patterns that he identified and the core issues he challenged us to address have become even more pressing than when he wrote.

This is a book for today because he wrote it for today.

In an effort to stimulate a much richer public dialogue Senator Cranston painted broad brushstrokes in his discussion of sovereignty in order to illustrate his main point:

> The prospects for humanity would be considerably brighter if, looking to the lessons of history for guidance, we were to set out consciously and deliberately to build a world community based upon democratic principles, upon the rights and responsibilities of its citizens, and upon the exercise of their individual sovereignty under the rule of law.

Cranston's themes ranged from the individual as the central basis of sovereignty and the authority of the state to UN reform. In light of his insights, I would like to reflect herein on some of the duties of nation-states to their own citizens and to the community of nations, peoples, and the living systems of the Earth. Such concerns were not paramount in 1648 when European states established the nation-state system through the Peace of Westphalia and thereby halted the Thirty Years War, quelling violence driven by religious fanaticism. Nor were they the primary concerns in 1945 when the UN system was established to ensure an end to wars of expansion and conquest.

The duty to protect the physical integrity of the state has always been a foundation of the legitimacy of state sovereignty. Senator Cranston places the individual at the center of granting authority to the state because he views the individual as the foundation of sovereignty. I would propose that the duty to protect individuals—citizens—is a basic duty of the state, and that the implications of this focus on human security include the duty to help citizens in other states in crisis and to ensure the viability of the global commons, the ecological systems upon which all lives depend.

The United Nations system ensures the legal identity and the equality of states by enshrining such status in Article 2.1 of the UN Charter, thus emphasizing stability, identity, and predictability, but setting very few standards of responsibility as part of that status. The sovereign state has the capacity to make authoritative decisions with respect to people and resources in its territory and can expect non-intervention from other states, with only several explicit exceptions. Those exceptions relate to the use of force in self-defense or when a state's conduct so offends international peace and security that the Security Council must intervene. Such offense is defined as "a threat to the peace, a breach of the peace or act of aggression."

The United Nations system builds upon three core elements of state sovereignty that were codified in 1933 in Uruguay at the Montevideo Convention on Rights and Duties of States. These included: a defined territory, a permanent population, and a functioning government.

In order to gain recognition in the UN system, virtually every state in the world has pledged to utilize international cooperation to solve problems of an economic, social, cultural, or humanitarian character and to promote and encourage respect for human rights and fundamental freedoms for all, without distinction of race, sex, language, or religion. This gives us norms of universal commitment that define the legitimate aspirations of states, but it gives us very little to explicitly define what happens when standards are not met.

The current barometer for measuring the success of states is increasingly being recognized exactly where Senator Cranston placed it—on individual human lives. Secretary General Kofi Annan's statement in the *Economist* of September 18, 1999, resonates with Senator Cranston's beliefs. Annan stated:

> State sovereignty, in its most basic sense, is being redefined—not least by the forces of globalization and international co-operation. States are now widely understood to be instruments at the service of their peoples, and not vice versa. At the same time individual sovereignty—by which I mean the fundamental freedom of each individual, enshrined in the Charter of the UN and subsequent international treaties—has been enhanced by a renewed and spreading consciousness of individual rights. When we read the Charter today, we are more than ever conscious that its aim is to protect individual human beings, not to protect those who abuse them.

This concept of the duty of the state to protect individuals is a long way from gaining the status of the responsibility to protect the physical integrity of the state. The United States, one of the world's most democratic countries, where liberty and freedom are high social values, is but one example of the extraordinary powers that are invested in the state in order to exercise its capacity to declare war and offer physical protection. For example, in the interest of national security, the US Congress has authority to:

> [C]ontrol the price of every commodity bought and sold within national boundaries; to fix the amount of rent to be charged for every room, home or building and this even though to an individual landlord there may be less than a fair return; to construct extensive systems of public works; to operate railroads; to prohibit the sale of liquor; to restrict freedom of speech in a manner that would be unwarranted in time of peace; to ration and allocate the distribution of every commodity important to the war effort; to restrict personal freedom of American citizens by curfew orders and the designation of areas of exclusion; and, finally, to demand of every citizen that he serves in the armed forces of the nation. (*Spaulding v. Douglas Aircraft Co.*, 154 F.2nd 419, 422–423 (9th Cir. 1946))

But the capacity of the state to exercise these and other powers can be forfeited if it does not fulfill a more basic and fundamental duty, a duty that supersedes sovereignty and goes to our common humanity. Before the General Assembly of the UN in 1999, and again in 2000, Secretary General Annan stated forcefully the essential dilemma:

> . . . if humanitarian intervention is, indeed, an unacceptable assault on sovereignty, how should we respond to a Rwanda, to a Srebrenica—to gross and systematic violations of human rights that affect every precept of our common humanity?

It is now internationally recognized that a state must protect its own people. It must not permit avoidable catastrophes such as mass murder, rape, or starvation. If it is unable or unwilling to do so, then others have a right and responsibility to intervene, even with force if necessary. George Soros in his article "The People's Sovereignty," in the January/February 2004 issue of *Foreign Policy*, sets forth a position deeply resonant with Senator Cranston's:

> But true sovereignty belongs to the people, who in turn delegate it to their governments. If governments abuse the authority entrusted to them and citizens have no opportunity to correct such abuses, outside interference is justified. By specifying that sovereignty is based on the people, the international community can penetrate nation-states' borders to protect the rights of citizens. In particular, the principle of the people's sovereignty can help solve two modern challenges: the obstacles to delivering aid effectively to sovereign states, and the obstacles to global collective action dealing with states experiencing internal conflict.

Such duties of humanitarian intervention were thoroughly addressed in a remarkable Commission of the Government of Canada—the International Commission on Intervention and State Sovereignty—that issued a report titled "Responsibility to Protect." As Secretary-General Annan stated upon the release of the report on February 15, 2002, it offers "a constructive shift away from debates about the 'right to intervene' towards the assertion of a 'responsibility to protect.'" The report thoroughly addresses questions such as: Do people suffering under intolerable conditions, which can be ameliorated through intervention, have a right to expect assistance? Should the sovereignty of the state in which they are living preclude other states from coming to offer help? Is there a duty to help? When does such a responsibility arise, and by and through what institutional structures can it be exercised? The report emphasized the same needs as Senator Cranston highlighted and for much the same reasons. Sovereignty should not be used as an absolute barrier to saving lives threatened by war and violence. As the Secretary-General said,

> What is clear is that when the sovereignty of States and the sovereignty of individuals come into conflict, we as an international community need to think hard about how far we will go to defend the former over the latter. Human rights and the evolving nature of humanitarian law will mean little if a principle guarded by States is always allowed to trump the protection of citizens within them.

A body of law is emerging to fortify the expectation of intervention of people suffering under illegitimate authority. It is based on the Human Rights provisions of the UN Charter, the Universal Declaration of Human Rights itself, the Genocide Convention, the Geneva Convention and its additional protocols on international humanitarian law, as well as the Statute of the International Criminal Court. The report of the International Commission on Intervention and State Sovereignty concluded that, based on the current status of international law, when a situation shocks the conscience because of large-scale loss of life—even without genocidal intent—or large-scale ethnic cleansing, killing, expulsion, or rape, and a state cannot prevent such disaster, then that state is simply not fulfilling one of its core sovereign functions. In such an instance multilateral coalitions, legally authorized through the UN system, can intervene to protect the citizens.

Providing for the health and security of citizens is the most basic duty of the state. If a state's conduct so fails these tests that its citizens cannot expect to survive, then common sense dictates that there is a serious problem that cannot be ignored. I suggest that the same analysis that places a duty on a state to protect its citizens from horrific violence also places a duty on the State to address quiet assaults on life caused by environmental factors. The fact that to address environmental factors requires multilateral cooperation does not detract from the sovereignty of each state but provides the only avenue available for each state to exercise its core function to protect its citizens. Thus, the core duty of the sovereign state to protect is not diminished but in fact fulfilled by strengthening multilateral institutions like the UN.

At a forum the Global Security Institute helped organize in the US Congress in October of 2003, UN Messenger of Peace Michael Douglas enumerated several issues that require all states to work together. He stated that universal cooperation is needed for

> ensuring bio-diversity and ending the destruction of thousands of species; reversing the depletion of fishing stocks; controlling ocean dumping; preventing ozone depletion; halting global warming; controlling and eliminating terrorism and weapons of mass destruction; fighting pandemic diseases; ending the tragedy of crushing poverty and lack of clean drinking water; and addressing crises arising from failed states. No nation or even a small group of nations can succeed in addressing these issues alone.

In fact, in order to protect citizens of any state, all states must cooperate in addressing these issues.

The World Wildlife Fund stated in a 1993 report that

> [h]umankind is only beginning to comprehend that its actions significantly affect biodiversity and that protection of biodiversity is a human responsibility. Left unchecked, human activities could eventually destroy the very habitat on which humankind depends.

But our very system of international production and commerce, if left unchecked and unregulated by governments, places our ecology at risk. It encourages corporate entities to place demands on ecological systems to gain market advantages, but passes the cost of injury to be shared by the whole.

The challenge of this process can be understood through the hypothetical model of the Tragedy of the Commons. In the example, cooperation and communication among the key actors is lacking. Shepherds bring their flock to a common grazing land. As long as no shepherd allows a flock to overgraze, the commons remain healthy. If one shepherd permits overgrazing then others will follow to similarly improve their economic situation. Since it would be irrational for an economic actor not to seek to maximize their economic advantage, reasonable behavior would encourage as much grazing as possible. Improving economic positioning is the most reasonable behavior for each individual actor. Ultimately, in the example, overgrazing renders the commons unable to regenerate rapidly enough to sustain the sheep, and thus all shepherds suffer. The tragedy in the story is not the callous nature of nature, but the incapacity of the decision makers to adequately address their collective interests and limit their individual conduct accordingly. Each was reasonable as a separate actor; collectively their conduct was unsustainable.

Excessive economic freedom to the detriment of environmental concerns is often protected by states saying that they do not want to enter into effective international environmental regimes because it will diminish their sovereignty. Thus, the practice of unregulated free market competition, without reference to ecological issues that demand responsible behavior, is injuring all citizens of all states by placing at risk the very foundations of a sustainable ecology.

The rules of the market cannot outwit the rules of biological regeneration. Marketplace freedom need not mean anarchy; we recognize numerous international legal regimes to regulate commerce. We must quickly respond to the ever-growing empirical evidence that the ecological systems of this precious finite planet are at risk. Incorporating responsible stewardship of the oceans, the ozone, and other aspects of the global commons does not mean diminishing sovereignty. In fact, it is the very fulfillment of the duty to protect inherent in the states' basic authority.

The fact that living systems and individual lives are interdependent cannot be ignored by states, which base their authority on their relative independence. This imperative of multilateralism is entirely new. Never before has the human community had the capacity to so injure the global commons and thus never before have we had to work so together, as Senator Cranston emphasizes, in order to survive.

If one nation does not join in a system to protect the oceans from dumping pollutants, others will use that nation's flag to dump. If one nation's fishing industry does not recognize the common interests of all to protect fish stocks, the very health of the oceanic system suffers. All must join together.

By focusing on one species in particular, the critical nature of the situation is highlighted. Horseshoe crabs, for example, are a wonder. They have been coming ashore and laying eggs the first full moon in June for about 400 million years, long before humans even gave June its name. They leave enough extra eggs for millions of birds to gorge themselves on their bounty, and thus ensure the viability of several species. Horseshoe crabs are one of only four in a class of creatures that are living relatives of ancient arachnids. Spiders and scorpions are in the same family.

But, as Sylvia Earle of the UN Environmental Program recently brought to public attention, horseshoe crabs are at risk. Lose one kind of horseshoe crab and a quarter of a genetic heritage is gone. Imagine if we lost a quarter of the insects, or flowering plants, or vertebrates. That is the magnitude of our negligence. Don't you suppose we might learn something, or at least respect a species, that has survived ice ages, major climactic changes, and upon which so many other beautiful creatures depend? Through over-fishing practices, this wonderful creature is placed at risk, as are so many others. Through such irresponsible practices, we place the ocean's health at risk. We are thus playing fast and loose with 97 percent of the planet's water and the ultimate source of much of the planet's life support system.

With techniques only decades old, gleaned from military sciences, we are able to find fish nearly anywhere, and, much like the example of the Tragedy of the Commons, actors maximize their market advantage to the ultimate detriment of the whole. With respect to the oceanic system, we don't know the consequences of warming it, polluting it, destroying entire species integrated with other species that live in it. We don't know the consequences of withdrawing hundreds of millions of tons of wild game, whether it be squid, tuna, creel, or clams. What might be a short-term gain for a few might spell disaster for us all. This serious risk should compel states to higher levels of cooperation in order to protect their own citizens

Many areas of the global commons require strengthened legal regimes. For example, the Vienna Convention and Montreal Protocol on protecting the ozone layer, the Convention on Long-Range Transboundary Air Pollution and its protocols, as well as numerous other legal instruments to protect citizens everywhere, are inadequately supported. Fishing stocks are not protected adequately. A better framing of the issue is to see that working together on ecological sustainability is as an expression of the duty of the state to protect its citizens. Failure in this area—ecocide—could be as serious as genocide in one state.

Another issue that affects the global commons relates to nuclear weapons. Their use cannot be contained in either space—because radiation travels—or time, since the weapons actually impact the human gene pool. Our collective security as a species is uniquely placed at risk by nuclear weapons. There is an imperative for cooperative security. Senator Cranston devoted most of his life to this issue.

He knew clearly that the greatest stimulant to the proliferation of nuclear and other weapons of mass destruction is the recalcitrance of the nuclear weapons states—particularly the United States—to negotiate their universal elimination. Although 182 states have renounced them, a handful continues to claim a unique right to possess and threaten to use them. This misplaced exercise of sovereignty and myopic pursuit of security continues to place all civilization in jeopardy. Thus tens of thousands of nuclear weapons remain with us.

The International Court of Justice unanimously called for a treaty to eliminate nuclear weapons, and in November 2003, at the 4th World Summit of Nobel Peace Laureates, a Statement was issued that stated:

> For some to say that nuclear weapons are good for them but not for others is simply not sustainable. The failure of the nuclear weapons states to abide by their legal pledge to negotiate the elimination of nuclear weapons, contained in the Nuclear Nonproliferation Treaty, is the greatest stimulus to their proliferation. Nuclear weapons are immoral and we call for their universal legal prohibition. They must be eliminated before they eliminate humanity.

By accident or design they will be used, and any use would be catastrophic. Senator Cranston often reminded us that pursuing security through the threat to annihilate millions of innocent people is unworthy of civilization.

Like environmental issues relating to the commons, if one nation does not adhere to the norm, the system breaks down. Thus, this collective threat is our opportunity to emphasize our common interest and our common concerns. By building relationships that reinforce cooperation in this area it makes it all the more easy to build in other areas.

Business works extremely well by forging trust and cooperation and striving for efficiency. But business is not in the business of ensuring a sustainable future for all citizens. Business will not protect the environment, and its model of unbridled competition is not appropriate for states charged with protecting the global commons. States alone have the capacity to fulfill that duty. States alone have the capacity to eliminate nuclear weapons.

These duties to protect require a revolution in the way we address sovereignty. Since it is based on individual responsibility, we as individuals have a responsibility to affirm the interdependence of life and to pressure the states in which we live to fulfill their common duties. Whether violence is the loud blast of a gun, the mushroom cloud, or the quiet destruction of the ecosystem, we are all responsible in different degrees and we can all make a difference.

Senator Alan Cranston calls us to this work because we also have a duty to live fully on possibly the only place in creation where love can thrive.

Jonathan Granoff

December 2003

# Source Notes

The following source notes for *The Sovereignty Revolution* are provided by Kim Cranston on the basis of Alan Cranston's notes and files. The numbers at left are page numbers in this volume.

11  *whose names sounded Jewish*: "Killings Illuminate Culture of White Supremacists," *New York Times*, 29 March 1998.

14  *a terrorist attack . . . on American soil . . . is "probable"*: "US faces 'quite real' threat of terrorist attack: Cohen," Yahoo Hong Kong News, 29 May 2000.

14  *It's not question of whether but when and where*: "The Coming War," NewsHour with Jim Lehrer, 25 August 1998.

14  *Horner, who commanded Allied Air Forces in the Gulf War*: Ambassador Tom Graham, conversation with author, Mexico, 2 February 1999.

14  *One of these days . . . What does the US do?*: "Arms Expert Warns U.S. Cities Face Nuclear Terrorism Threat," *Post Gazette*, 23 January 1999.

19  *Moynihan has pointed out . . . more than 60 percent of its territories*: Daniel Patrick Moynihan, *Pandemonium: Ethnicity in International Politics* (Oxford; Oxford University Press, 1993), 156.

25  *curious mix of shepherds and bomb throwers*: "Corsican Contradictions Charm and Vex France," *International Herald Tribune*, 8 September 1999.

27  *(Sovereignty's) birth is illegitimate . . . destructive of human values*: Louis Henkin, "Lecture, That 'S' Word: Sovereignty, and Globalization, and Human Rights, Et Cetera," *Fordham Law Review* 68 (October 1999), 1.

27  *The pervasiveness of that term . . . fictions upon fictions*: Louis Henkin, *International Law: Politics and Values* (Dordrecht and Boston: M. Nijhoff, 1995), 24–26.

29  *This myth . . . is fundamentally mistaken*: "Challenging the Necessity of Conflict," *The Christian Science Monitor*, 20 January 2000.

30  *independence, . . . impermeability and 'privacy'*: Louis Henkin, *International Law: Politics and Values* (Dordrecht and Boston: M. Nijhoff, 1995), 26.

30  *metaphors, fictions, fictions upon fictions*: Ibid.

34  *Beware the fury of the patient and long-suffering people*: "Rich-Poor Gap Endangers India, President Warns," *International Herald Tribune*, 26 January 2000.

34  *must be solved taking into account the human dimension, and not just the interests of investors*: "Havel Urges Multinationals to Heed the 'Voices of the People,'" *New York Times*, 23 August 2000.

35  *The biotech revolution . . . a common agreement on rules*: "We Are Increasingly Wired, but No One's in Charge," *International Herald Tribune*, 13–14 May 2000.

35  *The plain truth is . . . human rights abuses*: Pete Engardio with Catherine Belton, "Special Report: Global Capitalism: Can It Be Made to Work Better," *Business Week*, 6 November 2000, 74.

37  *We are aware. . . A global economy needs a global ethic*: Address to Board of Governors of International Monetary Fund, Prague, 26 September 2000.

37  *There can be no doubting . . . soiled her landscape*: *New York Times*, 26 August 2000.

38  *The nation-state is too big for the small problems and too small for the big problems*: Report on behalf of high-level expert group to Interaction Council, Vancouver, 19–22 May 1996.

39  *There has been a general . . . end of the nineteenth century*: "A Force Now in the World, Citizens Flex Social Muscle," *New York Times*, 10 July 1998, 15.

39  *a central feature of the political system*: "Political Brief: The People's Voice," *The Economist*, 14 August, 1999.

40  *the magistrate who exercised the sovereign power*: "James Madison Proposes Bill of Rights," Congressional Register, I, 423–37, and Gazette of the US, 10 and 13 June 1789.

40  *A sovereignty over sovereigns . . . is subversive of the order and ends of civil polity*: Federalist Papers #20, 11 December 1787.

41  *"We the people" instead of "We the states"*: Carl Van Doren, *The Great Rehearsal* (Penguin Books Australia Ltd., 1986), 219.

42  *"We are not forming coalitions between States" . . . "but union among people"*: Pascal Fontaine, *Europe in 10 Points* (European Commission, 1998).

44  *reflects a growing consciousness . . . at the European level*: "A European Identity: Nation-State Losing Ground," *New York Times*, 14 January 2000.

45  *it didn't have a telephone*: Ibid.

45  *a Europe of nation-states and a Europe of citizens*: John Rossant, "Commentary: The United States of Europe?," *Business Week*, 12 June 2000, 179.

49  *States do most of the governing in this country*: "Court and Congress," *New York Times*, 20 May 2000.

51  *at the hand of their own pathological, totalitarian, authoritarian or communist governments*: Gwyn Prins, "The Politics of Intervention," *Pugwash Occasional Papers*, vol. 1, no. 1 (February 2000), 55.

53  *The members of the UN . . . are legally committed to carry out its decisions*: Louis

Henkin, *Foreign Affairs and the U.S. Constitution* (Oxford University Press, 1996), 251.

56  *will turn outer space into a new weapon base and a battlefield*: Jenni Rissanen, "Gloom Hangs over CD," *British American Security Information Council BASIC REPORTS*, no. 74, 14 (August 2000), 2.

56  *This act is intended . . . claim of sovereignty*: Jeffrey T. Richelson, "Shootin' for the Moon," *The Bulletin of the Atomic Scientists*, September/October 2000, 23.

58  *national dignity and sovereignty*: Jon Lee Anderson, "Letters from Baghdad: The Unvanquished," *The New Yorker*, 11 December 2000, 79.

61  *every evil that the UN was founded to fight: . . . repression of women*: Editorial, *Wall Street Journal*, 9 October 2000.

67  *How citizenship will fare . . . is one of the great questions of our time*: *U.S. News and World Report*, 16–23 August 1999, 43.

67  *I regard myself as a citizen of the world as well as a citizen of the United States*: "Of Americans and the World," *International Herald Tribune*, 25 November 1999.

67  *I speak today as a citizen of the United States and of the world*: Ronald Reagan, Remarks in New York City Before the United Nations General Assembly Special Session Devoted to Disarmament, Reagan Library, Administration of Ronald Reagan, 784, 17 June 1982.

# About the Contributors

ALAN CRANSTON June 19, 1914–December 31, 2000

A graduate of Stanford University, Alan Cranston was a foreign correspondent for International News Service in Nazi Germany, Fascist Italy, and Ethiopia from 1936 to 1938. In 1939, he wrote and co-published a tabloid, anti-Nazi version of Adolf Hitler's *Mein Kampf* to awaken Americans to the fascist threat, and sold 500,000 copies for ten cents each before Hitler's publishers successfully sued him in US courts for copyright infringement and stopped its further distribution. Cranston served as Chief of the Foreign Language Division of the Office of War Information in the Executive Office of the President, 1942–44, and the US Army, 1944–45. He authored *The Killing of the Peace* (Viking) in 1945, which *The New York Times* rated one of the ten best books of 1945. Cranston was President of the United World Federalists from 1949 to 1952, President of the California Democratic Council from 1953 to 1958, and served as California State Controller from 1959 to 1967. Cranston was President of Homes for a Better America, a subsidiary of Kaufman-Broad Building Co., from 1967 to 1968, and Vice President of Carlsberg Financial Corp from 1968 to 1969. Elected for four terms, Alan Cranston served in the US Senate from 1969 to 1993, during which he was Democratic Whip and a member of the Foreign Relations, Intelligence, and Banking, Housing, and Urban Affairs Committees. After retiring from the Senate, Cranston served on the US-Kyrgyz Business Council, was a Senior International Advisor to Schooner Capital Corporation, and was an author, lecturer, and investor. In 1996 Cranston teamed with former Soviet President Mikhail Gorbachev as the chairman of the Gorbachev Foundation/USA, a San Francisco–based think-tank seeking nuclear disarmament. After serving five years as

Chairman of the Gorbachev Foundation/USA and the State of the World Forum, Cranston founded the Global Security Institute in 1999, a non-profit organization leading the international quest to eliminate nuclear weapons, and at the end of 2000 co-founded the Nuclear Threat Reduction Campaign. Cranston, an athlete all his life, was on the Stanford mile relay team—the fastest in the nation—in 1935 and in 1969 set a world record for 55-year-olds in the 100-yard dash, with a time of 12.6 seconds.

KIM CRANSTON

Kim Cranston is an investor and activist. Kim is Chair of the Global Security Institute, a member of the boards of the Social Venture Network and the Los Altos Community Foundation, an advisor to the Nuclear Threat Reduction Campaign, and a member of the California Committee North of Human Rights Watch. He also founded and manages the Institute for Organizational Evolution, which is developing Web-based approaches to enable people to collaborate more effectively to address a range of social and environmental challenges.

JANE GOODALL

Dr. Jane Goodall, DBE, began her groundbreaking study of chimpanzees in Gombe National Park, Tanzania, in June 1960. Her research, particularly the discovery that chimpanzees make and use tools, would redefine the relationship between humans and nonhumans. The study continues today as one of the longest uninterrupted studies of a wild animal group. Dr. Goodall earned her PhD in Ethology from Cambridge University in 1965. In 1977 she founded the Jane Goodall Institute, a global leader in the effort to protect chimpanzees and their habitats. The Institute also is widely recognized for establishing innovative community-centered conservation and development programs in Africa, and the Roots & Shoots® global youth program, which has groups in more than 87 countries. Dr. Goodall is a UN Messenger of Peace and an advisor to the Global Security Institute, and her honors include the Kyoto Prize, the Benjamin Franklin Medal in Life Science, and the 2003 Prince of Asturias Award for Technical and Scientific Research.

## MIKHAIL S. GORBACHEV

Mikhail Sergeyevich Gorbachev is President of the International Foundation for Socio-Economic and Political Studies (The Gorbachev Foundation)
based in Moscow and Green Cross International headquartered in Geneva,
and an advisor to the Global Security Institute. He was elected General Secretary of the Communist Party of the Soviet Union in March 1985 and President of the Soviet Union in March 1990. Mr. Gorbachev is the recipient of
the Nobel Peace Price (1990). He holds honorary doctorates from universities in Russia, the United States, and other countries.

## JONATHAN GRANOFF

Jonathan Granoff, Esq. is President of the Global Security Institute. For
more than twenty years he has contributed his legal expertise to the movement to eliminate nuclear weapons. His various roles include Vice President
of Lawyers Alliance for World Security, Vice President of the NGO Committee on Disarmament at the UN, and board positions with the Lawyers'
Committee on Nuclear Policy, among others. Mr. Granoff is also Co-Chair
of the American Bar Association, Committee on Arms Control and National
Security. He has lectured extensively all over the world on subjects relating
to peace, security, and human unity.

## JONATHAN SCHELL

From 1967 until 1987, Jonathan Schell was a staff writer and editor at
*The New Yorker* magazine. He was the principal writer of the magazine's
Notes and Comments, and also wrote long pieces, many of which were
published as books. They include *The Village of Ben Suc* (Knopf, 1967), *The
Fate of the Earth* (Knopf, 1982), and *The Time of Illusion* (Knopf, 1976). His
latest book is *The Unconquerable World: Power, Nonviolence and the Will of
the People* (Metropolitan Books 2003). From 1990 until 1996, Schell was a
columnist at Newsday and New York Newsday. He has taught at many
universities, including the Yale Law School, Emory University, New York
University, Princeton University, and Wesleyan University, where he was

a Distinguished Visiting Writer from 1997 to 2002. In 2002 he was a fellow at the Shorenstein Center on the Press, Politics, and Public Policy at the John F. Kennedy School of Government at Harvard. He is the Harold Willens Peace Fellow at the Nation Institute.